THEOLOGY, THIRD WORLD DEVELOPMENT AND ECONOMIC JUSTICE

THEOLOGY, THIRD WORLD DEVELOPMENT AND ECONOMIC JUSTICE

Edited by:
Walter Block and Donald Shaw

1985

Canadian Cataloguing in Publication Data

Main entry under title:

Theology, third world development and
    economic justice

    Proceedings of a conference held in
Regina, December, 1983.
    ISBN 0-88975-084-X

    1. Economics - Religious aspects -
Christianity - Congresses. ₂. Economic
development - Religious aspects -
Christianity - Congresses. 3. Liberation
theology - Congresses. 4. Developing
countries - Economic conditions -
Congresses. I. Block, Walter, 1941-
II. Shaw, Donald Elliott. III. Fraser
Institute (Vancouver, B.C.)
BR115.E3T54 1985   261.8'5   C85-091159-1

Printed in Canada.

CONTENTS

PREFACE

In the summer of 1983, representatives of the University of Regina, Campion and Luther Colleges, and the Centre for the Study of Economics and Religion (a division of the Fraser Institute) met to discuss plans for organizing a conference on questions of economics, ethics and religion. Panelists were picked, topics were set, a title was agreed upon, and on October 19, 1983, several thousand letters were mailed out inviting people, mainly from Saskatchewan, to attend.[*]

The conference, entitled "Theology, Third World Development and Economic Justice," was objected to by some Anglican, Roman Catholic and United Church clergymen, some labour unions, some university professors, Third World activists, and by some local community groups. The grounds were several: opposition to the inclusion of the Fraser Institute as a co-sponsor; fear that the panelists would not include representation across the political/economic spectrum; would exclude some religions; and that the sponsors would not invite distinguished theologians from Saskatchewan.

Controversy

Despite protests from these groups, the conference was held as scheduled. On December 4, 1983 several hundred people gathered at the University of Regina. They heard ten prominent clerics and academicians, organized into three panels, address themselves to issues of egalitarianism, economic justice, poverty, Third World development, unemployment, and the role of religion with respect to these phenomena.

---

[*]See Appendix A -- Editors

The co-sponsors of the event are publishing this monograph in order to be able to share the events of that day with a
wider audience. The following pages are a faithful representation of the dialogue which took place on that day. The text
reflects copy-editing only, in order to enhance readability; no
interpretations have been included by the co-editors. The
names of those who asked questions or made comments were
deleted, since we did not have permission to use them.
Several housekeeping details were deleted. This monograph is
therefore an accurate transcription of the events of December
4, 1983. With the record in front of them, readers can form
their own judgements concerning the controversy that accom-
panied the conference.

Walter Block, Vancouver
Donald Shaw, Regina

March, 1985

LORD PETER BAUER
Professor of Economics
London School of Economics

DR. WALTER BLOCK
Director, Centre for the Study of Economics and Religion;
Senior Economist, The Fraser Institute, Vancouver

DR. REX BODA
President, Canadian Bible College/
Canadian Theological Seminary, Regina

DR. WARD GASQUE
Vice-Principal and Professor of New Testament Studies
Regent College,
University of British Columbia, Vancouver

DR. JOSEPH B. GAVIN, S.J.
President, Campion College,
University of Regina, Saskatchewan

FATHER ISIDORE GORSKI
Professor of Humanities and Religious Studies
Campion College,
University of Regina, Saskatchewan

DR. PAUL HEYNE
Professor of Economics
University of Washington, Seattle

DR. RICHARD HORDERN
Assistant Professor of Religious Studies
Luther College,
University of Regina, Saskatchewan

DR. MURDITH MacLEAN
Warden of St. John's College
University of Manitoba, Winnipeg

FATHER JAMES SADOWSKY, S.J.
Professor of Philosophy and Ethics
Fordham University, New York

FATHER JAMES SCHALL, S.J.
Professor of Government and Political Philosophy
Georgetown University, Washington, D.C.

DR. DONALD E. SHAW
Vice President
University of Regina, Saskatchewan

DR. BERNARD ZAGORIN
Professor of History
University of Regina, Saskatchewan

OPENING REMARKS

WALTER BLOCK

WALTER BLOCK: I would like to get a few housekeeping details out of the way... because we are starting a few minutes earlier than scheduled. I wouldn't want to be unfair to people who are time watchers and arrived exactly on time. There will be a few changes in the order of the panels; as well, there will be a few replacement panelists.[*]

First of all, look at the Liberation Theology and Third World Development panel, that is, panel #1. It was originally scheduled to take place between 2:00 - 3:30 p.m. This is now panel #2, and will be pushed back to the 3:45 - 5:15 p.m. time slot. We will be switching, in other words, panel #1 and panel #2. We'll take what was panel #2, Religion, Egalitarianism and Economic Justice, which was originally scheduled from 3:45 - 5:15 p.m., and move it to the 2:00 - 3:30 p.m. slot (God willing and the microphones willing).

On the first panel, which is now Religion, Egalitarianism and Economic Justice, the following changes are made. Donald Shaw will be the Chairman, but for panelists, please cross out Dr. Judith Alexander and Dr. Terry Anderson and replace them with Dr. Ward Gasque. Dr. Paul Heyne and Father James Sadowsky will remain on what is now the first panel.

The second panel, which will now be Liberation Theology and Third World Development, will be chaired by Dr. Bernard Zagorin who replaces Dr. Roland E. Miller, and will consist of Lord Peter Bauer, Dr. Murdith MacLean, and, instead of Professor Douglas MacArthur, Professor Rick Hordern.

----
[*]See Appendix B -- Editors

The third panel, I am happy to say, stays in its pristine form with the same panelists and the same time slot. I hope that will go on as we had hoped that it would.

That's it for the housekeeping remarks. I would like now to address some more substantive matters.

Protest

As anyone aware of the newspaper, radio and television accounts in Saskatchewan knows, a controversy has arisen concerning the propriety of holding this conference on economics, ethics and religion. Had this not occurred, I had intended to tell, in some detail, why we are holding the conference, why we thought it important, and what we hoped to accomplish. But, given the controversy, I will limit this account to a very brief statement on these matters.

The Canadian Conference of Catholic Bishops published, at the beginning of this year, a statement called, Ethical Reflections on the Economic Crisis. In that short document, on no less than three different occasions, they called for meaningful dialogue. I, for one, can't believe that meaningful dialogue should be confined to people of like-minded views. In my opinion, there is certainly room in the concept of meaningful dialogue for exchanges of ideas among people with different points of view. In making up our invitation list to this conference we tried to include people with contrary points of view, including scholars, academics, clergymen, theologians, and economists. We wanted to bring them together to have a dialogue on important questions of the day in economics and theology. The titles of the panels indicate that we have picked three important issues in this field.

That's what I would have said. Under ordinary circumstances, I would have elaborated on these points. Instead, what I want to do now is spend a little time describing the Fraser Institute, since its very status has been called into question by the controversy.

The Fraser Institute is a research organization which studies public policy issues and reports on this work in a style comprehensible to the average Canadian. We have published some 50 different books on many of the aspects of public

policy that affect Canadians. Yes, we do try to obtain
publicity for these studies. We feel that if we do the research
but hide it under a bushel, it will do the Canadian public no
good at all. So we publish the books in attractively packaged
covers. We talk about them on radio and television and we try
to promote this research to the Canadian people.

Rent Control

I think it's very important that we funnel what would otherwise be esoteric information to the Canadian people because
they can benefit. One example is rent control. The Fraser
Institute has been widely castigated in the Regina press for
opposing rent control. We did a study called Rent Control:
Myths and Realities, which considers the rent control experience of eight different countries over the last 50 years. The
authors of this volume were very prestigious, and included
three Nobel prize winners: Milton Friedman, George Stigler,
and Friedrich Hayek. But some people dismiss these economists as "right-wingers," or Fascists, or fiends, who only want
to grind down the poor, and who are thus evil incarnate. What
then can we think of the following statements, not by people
associated with the right-wing or free market, but with the
leftish causes? I want to read to you two interesting quota-
tions, also cited in Rent Control: Myths and Realities, from
people who have no way, manner, shape or form of association
with what might be considered the right wing, or conservativ-
ism, or free enterprise. The first one is another Nobel prize
winner, Gunnar Myrdal, an important architect of the Swedish
Labour Party's welfare state, who says: "Rent control has in
certain Western countries constituted maybe the worst example of poor planning by governments lacking courage and
vision."

Another commentary is from a second socialist econo-
mist--Assar Lindbeck. Says he, "In many cases rent control
appears to be the most efficient technique presently known to
destroy a city, except for bombing." This is hardly a ringing
endorsement of rent control from people with clear creden-
tials on the left side of the political spectrum.

Balanced Dialogue

One of the divisions of the Fraser Institute is the Centre for the Study of Economics and Religion, of which I have the honour to be Director, as well as Senior Economist in the overall Fraser Institute. Our division holds conferences and also publishes books. Many of our activities are balanced with representation of all sides of the political spectrum. For example, we have a book coming out soon which will include as authors Gregory Baum and Primate Ted Scott of the Anglican Church, who are not known as radical free enterprisers, to say the least. As well, we include the work of some two dozen people in these books evenly balanced along the left-right spectrum; there is absolute egalitarianism in this sense.

I want to read you a list of some of the people whom we have invited to this present Regina Conference in an attempt to achieve a balance--to have a meaningful dialogue. They are: Ben Smillie, St. Andrew's College of Saskatoon; Bishops Remy DeRoo and Proulx of the Catholic Church; John Richards, presently an Economics Professor at Simon Fraser University, and a former NDP MLA from Saskatoon; Gregory Baum from St. Michael's; Bob Ogle, a federal NDP MP; Michael Peers, an Anglican Archbishop; Ted Scott, Anglican Primate; Terry Anderson, a United Church Professor of Social Ethics at the Vancouver School of Theology; David Lockhead, a Marxist theologian also at the Vancouver School of Theology; Archbishop Halpin of the Catholic Diocese; Rod Booth of the Information Office of the United Church; Judy Alexander of the Economics Department of the University of Regina; Arthur Krentz, Philosophy Professor of Luther College; Ian Rennie and Douglas Webster, both of Ontario Theological School in Willowdale; Mack Watt, of the University of Winnipeg Religious Department and James Wall, the Editor of Christian Century.

This is a clear indication that we tried to balance the panelists in order to have a meaningful dialogue. Yet in the controversy surrounding this conference it has been claimed that the Institute is biased, right wing, and is interested only in proselytizing and achieving monopoly of the microphone. Such a contention cannot be maintained by reasonable people.

Affiliations

What else has the Fraser Institute accomplished? Well, one result is that some of our books have been widely adopted for classroom use, across Canada and the United States. We have as authors many members from the faculties of a broad spectrum of the universities and colleges in Canada. I mention this because of the allegation made by some protesters that a co-sponsorship between the University of Regina and The Fraser Institute would be unique, representing an untoward grant of prestige from the former to the latter. I would like to read to you a list of the universities, other than the University of Regina, which have been associated with us in the past, either by adopting our books, or by lending us their professors to do research for the Fraser Institute, or by co-sponsoring previous Centre for the Study for Economics and Religion conferences on economics and religion or other topics. Universities associated with us in this way include: McGill; McMaster; Queen's; Simon Fraser; Alberta; British Columbia; Saskatchewan; Lethbridge; Calgary; Guelph; Manitoba; Ottawa; Quebec; Toronto; P.E.I.; Victoria; Waterloo; Western Ontario; York; Wilfrid Laurier; and Ryerson Polytechnic. In addition, in the United States, there are Columbia; Dartmouth; Massachusetts Institute of Technology; Rutgers; Tufts; University of Virgina; University of Washington; Williams College; Brown; Harvard; and numerous other smaller institutions.

Thirdly, requests of the Fraser Institute have been made from the following publishing houses to reprint parts of our studies in their own books: Gage; Prentice-Hall; McGraw-Hill Ryerson; University of Western Ontario, School of Business; Harper and Row; UBC Faculty of Commerce; Xerox; Holt Rinehart Winston; U.S. Joint Economic Committee; Kendall Hunt; Scott Foresman; University of North Carolina Press; and the University of Alberta.

Publicity

People are interested in hearing more about our research and we try to comply. We do so by making regular radio and television appearances -- my colleague, Mike Walker, to a greater degree, and myself to a lesser degree. We have columns in the <u>Financial Post</u>, <u>Grainews</u>, <u>Province</u> and the <u>Sterling</u> syndicated newspaper chain, a total of some 50 different newspapers in all.

We also give speeches -- have mouth, will travel! We have given speeches to civic groups such as the Rotary, the Chamber of Commerce, universities, colleges, high schools, business corporations, trade associations, clergy, teachers, journalists, and even politicians. This is where another problem in the present controversy came up. Let me mention the political institutions that we have spoken to or had such dealings with. They include the Progessive Conservatives, the Liberals, the Socreds, the NDP, the Libertarians, parliamentary committees, government caucuses, Operation Solidarity, Solidarity Coalition of B.C. and even card-carrying Communists. In May, the Bill Bennett Socred government of B.C. invited Dr. Michael Walker, the Director of the Fraser Institute, to give it the benefit of his opinions; one of the things that he advocated, as he has advised all through the length and breadth of Canada, is that rent control is not a good idea, it's not in the interests of the Canadian people. A few months later, Bill Bennett saw fit to adopt this advice. I say now, and I say it loud and clear, that if asked, we will give advice to anyone who asks us of whatever political persuasion. We'll go to Nova Scotia, Ontario, Saskatchewan, anywhere. We are a Canadian research institution and we make our research available to all those who ask us -- of whatever political stripe, whether they are politicians or members of any part of Canadian society. To the degree that our advice is accepted, the Canadian people will tend to benefit, in my opinion, especially the poor.

Budget

One more word about the Fraser Institute: 58 per cent of its budget is met by large-scale businesses. The rest of it is derived from small businesses, individuals, groups, partnerships, and foundations. We are castigated on this ground for being mouth-pieces of businessmen. I say that this is false. We have criticized wage controls, a measure favoured by the business community several years ago during the era of the Anti Inflation Board. But our opposition to wage controls was compatible with the view of the union sector. We are on record as favouring voluntary communes. We did a study on the Hutterites, which is a Communalist religious group in Alberta which is being persecuted, and we defended them. We have opposed many business-advocated positions such as bail-outs, tariffs, subsidies, licenses, and special privileges for corporations. As a result of authoritative research, the work of our eminent and prestigious authors, we have come to the position that the marketplace is in the best interests of the Canadian people. This is not the same thing as saying that we favour business. We favour business in the abstract, in the sense of business's right to do business. We certainly do not favour special privileges for particular businesses. That's a very different point of view.

It is now my honour to introduce you to Don Shaw, a man who needs no introduction in Regina, of course, or anywhere in Canadian academic circles either. He is the Vice-President of the University of Regina, a man of steadfast devotion to the concept of intellectual competition, to academic freedom and to the free market in ideas.

OPENING REMARKS

DON SHAW

DON SHAW: Ladies and Gentlemen, Mr. Minister. Mr. Lorne Hepworth is here representing the Premier at the Conference and we welcome you sir.

Ladies and gentlemen, we thank you very much for attending the conference. I extend to you, as participants in the conference, a very warm welcome from the University of Regina, the entire university community, including Campion College and Luther College. The University of Regina has a special relationship with its federated colleges, of which Campion and Luther are two. (The third is the Saskatchewan Indian Federated College which is not involved in this particular conference.)

Walter, you've made a difficult job for the Chairman because you have just taken all my time in your address! Dr. Block has referred to the controversy that has arisen over this conference. That doesn't bother me at all. It doesn't bother my colleagues Dr. Gavin, the President of Campion College, or Dr. Anderson, the President of Luther College. This is because we believe in freedom of expression. We have co-sponsored this event on the assumption that by so doing we have an opportunity to influence whatever proceedings may emerge from the conference. Indeed Walter and I have discussed it and we will do just that. Walter and I will be co-editors of any proceedings to emerge. I have reserved the right to consult with any of my colleagues on the contents of the proceedings.

Endorsement

I think the other thing that needs to be said, once again, is that co-sponsorship does not involve endorsement of the views of our co-sponsors. Indeed, it would be difficult for Campion College, which is the Roman Catholic college, and for Luther College, which is the Lutheran college, to endorse entirely each other's philosophical points of view. I repeat, co-sponsorship does not mean endorsement. It does mean that we think the topic is worthy of public discussion, to free and open discussion. I reaffirm the solidarity of the University of Regina and Campion College and Luther College in continuing to sponsor the conference despite some opposition. The opposition, by the way, was not overwhelming. There is a large element within the University of Regina community, including Campion College and Luther College, which supports very strongly the co-sponsorship.

I would ask that all audience comments be confined to the subject at hand. This is not the place to discuss the fact of co-sponsorship. I hope that this subject will not be raised on the floor today. That is not the purpose of this conference. I am quite willing to discuss the matter with anybody who wishes to get in touch with me after the conference, and I am sure that Dr. Gavin of Campion College and Dr. Anderson of Luther College are also prepared to do so.

I would like to extend a special thank you to Professors Rick Hordern, Bernie Zagorin, and Ward Gasque, who have agreed to serve either as Chairmen or panelists on late notice. I think it is noteworthy that they have done so, and certainly I appreciate that very much.

Control of Conference

Let me mention a couple of specific issues that have come up. The first was a specific criticism that had been made within the University. It was that the order of the panelists and control of the proceedings was being determined by the Fraser Institute. That is not true. The order of appearance of the panelists has been determined by the Chairmen of the panels, all of whom are members of the University of Regina or Federated Colleges. The control of the proceedings is the role of the Chairmen. The Chairmen are not going to enter into the debate. The Chairmen are here only to maintain order within the conference.

One other comment that I believe I should make is that the University of Regina and Luther College and Campion College have not been associated in any way with the private or invitational conference which was sponsored by the Fraser Institute and which preceded this open conference today. That is not meant as criticism or endorsement. It is simply a statement of fact.

Apology

As well, there has been some confusion with respect to the panelists on the programme and in particular Dr. Judith Alexander and Professor Douglas MacArthur of the Economics Department of the University. They have declined to serve as panelists, and in fairness to them I must state publicly that there was a foul-up, for which I will take personal responsibility. There was a break in communication between my office and the conference office, in that letters of invitation to them were not issued prior to the issuance of the printed programme. And for that I apologize. I also accept the responsibility for it.

There have been statements appearing or aired in the media concerning Professor MacArthur. I wish to state publicly again that the University of Regina considers Professor MacArthur to be a highly valued, respected, and reliable member of the academic community.

There will be two audience microphones. There is one in this aisle and one in that aisle. I will ask members of the audience to use them when they have questions or comments to make of the panelists. I have retained, after meeting with the other two Chairmen of the three sessions, the right to cut off the microphones, if need be. I hope we won't have to do it. But in order to involve as many participants as would like to be involved in the discussion it may be necessary to do so.

My final comment is that each panelist is restricted to a 10 - 12 minute presentation. The Chairmen reserve the right to give a two-minute warning to the panelists.

Having said those things, I simply say again, welcome to the conference. We encourage as much audience participation as possible, and ample time for this has been allotted. The Chairmen have agreed to alternate access to the microphones from that side -- to this side -- my left, my right. That will be the order of presentation. I hope that we will have an open and free discussion and I look forward to the comments that will come today.

Thank you.

RELIGION, EGALITARIANISM AND ECONOMIC JUSTICE

DR. WARD GASQUE

DON SHAW: I invite the members of the first panel, Dr. Paul Heyne, Father James Sadowsky and Dr. Ward Gasque to come to the stage now, please. The first panel is entitled, Religion, Egalitarianism and Economic Justice.

The order in which the panelists will appear to discuss their points of view on this topic will be -- Dr. Ward Gasque first, Dr. Paul Heyne second, and Father James Sadowsky, third. That is in alphabetical order and there is believe me, no philosophical or political view attached to that! (laughter) Dr. Gasque, as I said before, agreed late in the game to become a panelist, and I thank you again for that sir.

Dr. Gasque is the Vice-Principal and Professor of New Testament Studies at Regent College in Vancouver. He did his doctorate at Manchester University in England. He is a former Editor-at-Large of Christianity Today and the author of two books and many essays. As well, he is the editor of four collections of scholarly essays and co-editor of the Good News Bible Commentary and the New International Greek Text Commentary. I will now turn the microphone over to you Dr. Gasque. If that one doesn't work, I'll give you another one. These microphones require that one be very close to them.

WARD GASQUE: I shall be looking at the subject, Religion, Equality and Economic Justice. Since I am a Biblical scholar, theologian, and committed to a Christian position (not that my position is the Christian position) I shall try to think Christian-ly about this subject. I would like to begin by sketching some biblical pre-suppositions that a Christian theologian might find of interest in the discussion. I would like to start with Jesus and the Gospels. One of the things that strikes the student of the New Testament who seeks to read the words of Christ and to rivet his attention on them is the concern that Jesus has for the poor and -- conversely -- the warnings which he gives to the rich. At my morning Bible reading, I read in Luke, Chapter 6, "And Jesus said, blessed are you who are poor, for yours is the Kingdom of God. Blessed are you who hunger now, for you will be satisfied." And conversely, "but woe to you who are rich for you are receiving your comfort in the here and now. Woe to you who are well-fed for you will be hungry."

I once had the responsibility of giving a series of expositions of the Gospel according to Luke to an affluent Canadian congregation, and I kept hoping that somewhere in the Gospel Jesus would say something nice about rich people. (laughter) He doesn't. At most, there are a couple of references which might be interpreted as neutral about wealthy people. Rather, He says nice things about the poor, and shows much concern for them. He is constantly warning the wealthy about the danger of their wealth and the abuse of the power that wealth gives us. This is something to which believing Christians must listen.

Love for Neighbour

The second biblical principle is the ethical maxim that Jesus also lays down as fundamental. He quotes, of course, from the Old Testament, to the effect that one has the responsibility to show love for one's neighbour. We think of His classic parable of the good Samaritan. The good Samaritan, who would be despised by the people to whom Jesus is talking, becomes the hero. The priest and the Levite are more concerned with what is good theology and good religious practice. They go up to Jerusalem, to the temple, to do their bit, and they pass by and neglect this poor wounded man on the roadside. The Samaritan stops to help. He acts, rather than simply talks. He shows concern, he shows love to his neighbour.

A third important concept involves the Christian tradition that there are sins of omission as well as sins of comission. That is to say, people are guilty not simply of doing things expressly forbidden or expressly evil, but also of neglecting to do what is right. Therefore, moral people, certainly Christian people, have a concern to take positive steps. They must not simply refrain from defrauding people or taking advantage of people or making people poor. They have an obligation to help those who are needy. The judgement of God, according to the teaching of our Lord, comes upon those who do not visit the prisoners, who do not clothe the unclothed, who do not feed those who are hungry.

Creation

Another doctrine from the teaching of scripture is important-- the Christian doctrine of creation. Here we hark back to the early chapters of Genesis where man is made in the image of God, where the created order is good, and where man (as male and female) is placed in the world to be a steward, to represent God, to tend for the created order. All possessions, including this earth, are possessed temporarily. Ultimately, God is the owner and man is simply the steward, His vice-regent to look after God's property. Therefore, the biblically oriented Christian sees private property as something held in trust, something that a person has been entrusted with by God. The Christian thus has a responsibility before God to use private property for His glory and to thus share it with others.

Finally, I would point out that the Old Testament provides certain models. It is not sufficient to be honest and fair and just, and not to take advantage of people but to do concrete things that really help to establish some degree of equality, or tendencies towards equality, in society. We think of things like the laws of the gleanings. In the Old Testament days, it was against the law for a farmer to harvest everything in his garden or field. He had to leave some produce around the edges for the poor. Again, we think of the sabbatical law by which, in every seven years, debts were generally wiped out. People who had sold themselves into slavery were freed. And then, of course, the culmination of this practice took place in ancient Israel on the new jubilee every 50 years. Then, even land was restored to its original owners as well as all debts being wiped out on the new jubilee every 50 years in ancient Israel.

These are a few biblical principles that I think are important for a Christian when dealing with this subject.

DON SHAW, CHAIRMAN: Thank you, Dr. Gasque. I didn't even have to invoke the two minute limit on you.

RELIGION, EGALITARIANISM AND ECONOMIC JUSTICE

DR. PAUL HEYNE

DON SHAW, CHAIRMAN: We will delay discussion, questions and comments until all three panelists have completed their addresses. The next speaker is Dr. Paul Heyne, who is a Professor of Economics at the University of Washington in Seattle. Dr. Heyne has a Ph.D. in Theology from the University of Chicago. He is the author of Private Keepers of the Public Interest and of a college economics text (which has sold very well), entitled, The Economic Way of Thinking. I might say, Paul, that Private Keepers of the Public Interest is one that in the dear, dead days when I still did a fair amount of teaching, I used as a reference in my classes on Business and Society. Dr. Heyne, you have the floor.

PAUL HEYNE: Thank you. I'm glad these microphones aren't too sensitive because I missed lunch and my stomach is growling. (laughter)

I'm going to stick very closely to the notes that I wrote out for this so that I will get through in 11½ minutes. All arguments have to begin somewhere. I am going to begin with the pre-supposition that justice is the first virtue of social systems. I think I could defend that with reference to political philosophers of all stripes, with reference to the Old and New Testaments, and from an examination of how societies function and change and disappear. But I don't want to defend it. I want to assume it in order to get on with reasons and questions and to offer some suggestions about the pursuit of justice in our times, in our societies --especially the pursuit of justice by religious people.

I am going to use a text. I hadn't planned to, but when I went to church this morning the Old Testament lesson was just too appropriate. Here it is from Isaiah 11, "There shall come forth a shoot from the stump of Jessie and the branch shall grow out of His roots and the spirit of the Lord shall rest upon Him. The spirit of wisdom and understanding, the spirit of council and might, the spirit of knowledge, and the fear of the Lord and His delight shall be in the fear of the Lord. He shall not judge by what His eyes see, or decide by what His ears hear, but with righteousness He shall judge the poor and decide with equity for the meek of the earth."

This is a stirring vision of a coming reign of perfect justice. Why is it perfect? Let me call your attention to some words here. "He shall not judge by what His eyes see, or decide by what His ears hear. He will judge with equity for the meek of the earth." He is going to judge with perfect justice. He is not going to be limited, this coming ruler, this coming Messiah, by the limitations of human knowledge. I want to stress that because this is not what we are called to do. That is my contention. That includes those of us who wish to be obedient to the biblical imperative. We must judge by what our eyes see and by what our ears hear; in other words, by what we can know.

Imperfect Knowledge

It is important, I think, to recognize that we know very little. We do not know, for example, what people really deserve. I have to assign grades, each term, to as many as 700 students. I do not pretend to assign them on the basis of true merit. I assign them on the basis of performance on my exams, which is only imperfectly correlated with what students actually know about the subject. It is even less closely correlated with what they learn in the course, and it is not at all connected, as far as I can tell, with what they truly deserve as unique human beings.

Yet I would contend that I am rating justly -- not with perfect justice, not with divine justice. I don't possess the perfect or divine knowledge and impartiality which that would require. I aim at human justice. And human justice, because we are humans and not gods, must content itself with the avoidance of injustice. I avoid injustice in assigning grades by following the rules. The rules which I try to make explicit at the beginning of the term, in advance, include: three tests and one paper, evaluated by such-and-such procedures and then converted into grades on the basis of such-and-such a calculation. I lay those rules down in advance in the syllabus. But I also have to follow some other rules that are implicit, that are passive, that are just taken for granted, which can't even be completely spelled out. But they are rules that the students take for granted. For example, tests will be evaluated by competent examiners. I don't turn their papers over to my six year old daughter for evaluation. (laughter) No credit will be given for physical beauty. No deduction will be made for wearing punk hair styles. (laughter) Questions will relate to the material of the course. I don't put any of that in the syllabus, but it is all taken for granted.

Go By the Rules

My central thesis is that in a world of human beings with limited knowledge and partial perspectives, justice requires, above all, that we go by the rules. What rules? The rules to which we have committed ourselves -- rules which others expect us to follow because we have committed ourselves to them.

I must ask you to test this out in your own experience. When somebody says, "What is justice?," we shrug our shoulders. What is justice? Who is to say? But we can and do recognize injustice. We often say, "that's not fair." We say this with conviction as if it really is unfair, unjust. We don't ask who is to say when we are talking about injustice. I'm to say. "I'm telling you, that's not fair." What do we mean? What do you mean? What are we talking about in such situations? Again, I ask you to refer to your own experience. Think of situations in which you have said, "that's not right. That's not just. That's not fair." I think what we are doing is saying, "somebody broke the rules that apply in this situation." Injustice is done when someone is hurt because someone else, an individual or a group, failed to follow the rules. The rules make up our social contract. They are the whole set of promises that we have given to one another, explicitly and implicitly. They comprise our obligations to one another. And obligations create rights.

Rights Violations

Injustice is done to you when your rights are violated. And your rights are what you may legitimately expect from others because they have promised, they have committed themselves. Therefore, you have relied upon them. I am suggesting that injustice, human injustice, is promise-breaking. Social justice, human social justice, and therefore the social justice that religious people too should respect because they are also human, requires we be faithful to the vast, complex, ever-changing, but mostly unchanging promises that we make to one another. We do so by living together in common societies -- by forming families, taking on tasks, accepting employment, enrolling in schools, buying a house, investing in a business, casting a vote, paying taxes, or driving a car. Just think about all the promises you make when you get into a car and start to drive. Heading the list is the promise that you haven't been drinking.

I am talking about justice. Justice is not love. Love requires justice. But justice does not exhaust the content of love. However, I think love does prohibit injustice. It prohibits unjust treatment of others. I believe that the first obligation of love is to avoid injustice, including injustices done to some with the intention of showing love to others. In the 20th century I think it has again become terribly important to remember the evil that good men do -- to recall how much suffering has been inflicted in human history and is being inflicted today, right now, in the name of religion and ideology. Good intentions are not enough when they are the intentions of finite human beings. Having religious faith doesn't change that.

DON SHAW, CHAIRMAN: Dr. Heyne, thank you very much. Thank you also for staying within the time limits that we established. We are setting a good pace here.

RELIGION, EGALITARIANISM AND ECONOMIC JUSTICE
FATHER JAMES SADOWSKY

DON SHAW, CHAIRMAN: The next panelist is Father James Sadowsky, who is a member of the Society of Jesus. He is a Professor of Philosophy and Ethics at Fordham University in New York. Father Sadowsky is the author of Transubstantiation and Scholastic Philosophy: Private Property and Collective Ownership. He has been a contributor to the American Catholic Philosophical Review. We are very pleased to have you with us, Father Sadowsky, and the floor is yours, sir.

JAMES SADOWSKY: In a book called The State, Franz Oppenheim tells us that there are two different paths to enrichment. There is the economic way of enrichment and there is the political way of enrichment. We can only defend the economic means of enrichment. This comes about as a result of voluntary exchange; it is entered into because both parties expect to benefit by it. This, in other words, is trade.

The political means of enrichment consists basically of gaining wealth by exploitation. That is, one becomes rich not by exchanging what one has for what somebody else has, but simply by taking from somebody what he has produced. This enrichment is parasitical of the peaceful production of others and parasitical of the economic means of enrichment. I say "parasitical" because we can readily see that there could be no political enrichment if it were not for economic enrichment. If the people don't produce, then there is nothing the thief can take.

I think this is relevant to what we read about riches in the Bible, indeed in the early Christian church. This is the period which precedes the development of a regime of voluntary exchanges. Almost all the riches of that day, it strikes me, were suspect -- in almost every case they were gained as the result of extraction or exploitation. In other words, one could almost assume that a rich person was either the extractor of goods from somebody else, or at least the possessor of goods that had been previously taken from others. The idea that "property is theft" thus applied, all too often in the time of the Bible. But to apply this idea to a society in which individuals become rich as a result of the economic means of enrichment is perhaps anachronistic.

Consider the good Samaritan. I have no doubt that we are obliged to help those in need. Indeed, I think that not to do so is a sin. I don't think, however, that failing to do so is a crime: that is, the law has no right to force others to act as good Samaritans. What would one have thought of the good Samaritan if instead of helping the wounded man, he had forced others to do so at the point of a gun? (laughter)

Voluntary Transactions

It is illegitimate to use force to bring an unwilling participant into any transaction. Insofar as people abstain from such concern, however, they are not violating the rights of others. Those who do not approve of any association or transaction, have the right not to participate. But they don't have the right to stop consenting adults from engaging in mutually beneficial trade.

To say that the market is unjust is essentially to claim the right to ban voluntary transactions. A free society does not forbid people to set up communal arrangements. They are perfectly welcome to do so. They may not find it to their advantage to do so. They may find it more advantageous to flee into the market; but that surely is not the fault of those who are already market participants. It is, however, characteristic of the socialistic approach that it would not allow the existence of consenting capitalists. They do not allow free economic exchanges to take place. And it is no accident that in Russia, for example, the largest category of crime is what is called economic crime. But these economic crimes, of course, are nothing but exchanges that take place between consenting adults.

My defense of the market is the notion of voluntary exchange, precisely, the right to associate with people or not to associate with them. Behind all this is the right to property. According to this theory, people have the right to own possessions which are exclusively theirs -- in the sense that other people do not have the right forcibly to separate them from their possessions.

How does one acquire private property beyond that piece of property with which all of us are born, namely our own human bodies? One acquires private property by helping himself to that which was previously unkown; for example, by taking an apple off the tree, or by cultivating land that hitherto was not cultivated. That is the way private property arises. If one says, "you can't do this," then such a person is really claiming to have the right to control what I just took and therefore he is acting improperly. But his claim would have validity, it seems to me, only if this were his own private property. Then the question arises, how did it become this person's private property since he or she did nothing to get it? Thank you.

DON SHAW, CHAIRMAN: Thank you Father Sadowsky. As one who has taught in the area of business and society for many years, I find it extremely difficult to bite my tongue and not become involved. That is not a comment on your talk but rather on the whole subject.

RELIGION, EGALITARIANISM, AND ECONOMIC JUSTICE

DISCUSSION

DON SHAW, CHAIRMAN: The game rules for participation by the audience are as follows. I will ask members of the audience to use the microphones in the two outside aisles and will ask them to make their questions or comments as brief as possible. I hope it won't be necessary to cut off any microphones. We will start first on this side, and if you have a question or a comment, please step to the microphone. I don't see a rush to that side. Is there somebody over here who would like to make a question or a comment? Would you please identify yourself? It is not necessary but not undesirable either if one identifies not only his name but his association.*

SPEAKER #1: I am a faculty member of the Department of Political Science at the University of Regina. My question is addressed to Dr. Paul Heyne. His principal thesis is that injustice can be avoided by committing oneself or the society to the rules. On the surface this appears to be an extremely good principle. But at the same time it perplexes me, and for two reasons.

First, if the rules are just, then the premise is all right. If the rules are not just, then the premise has no basis.

----

* For purposes of confidentiality, the names of the speakers have been deleted. -- Editors

Secondly, suppose that the rules were the rules of the Republic of South Africa. This would mean that we are committed to the preservation of apartheid there. Following Heyne's prescription, one would be committed to the preservation of colonialism wherever it exists. We are also committed to inequality in those parts of Canada where it exists. All this is true unless your interpretation of the rules is along other lines. For example, it could be natural rights or natural justice, or those rules which are based on the precepts of the Bible. Of course, the Bible is not the religion of all -- probably only three-fourths of the population of the world. Would you please clarify your point?

PAUL HEYNE: I wouldn't like to clarify it, but I'd better. (laughter) At least I had better try. Yours is the most powerful question that should be asked of my position and I am going to try to answer it briefly. Let me begin it by turning the question around. Suppose we lived in a society where the laws are unjust. Of course, the laws are a part of the rules, a very important part of the rules. I would ask, how would we know that? How would you and I know that? If nobody knows it, it is irrelevant. But my answer would be that we would know that by comparing those laws with something more basic. I am reluctant to talk about South Africa. I would really like to talk about Canada. Unfortunately, I am a citizen of the United States, and I know more about that country. In both the United States and Canada there are constitutions which govern laws. But more importantly, I think, beneath and beyond those constitutions there are the moral rules. There is the moral consensus which judges use, which legislators use in interpreting the Constitution. It is this to which we refer in condemning some laws or social practices as unjust.

Let me give just one example from the United States. It involved Martin Luther King. When he began his activities, he made the claim that some of the promises that people in the United States had made to each other were bad promises. They should not have been made. For example, the state of Georgia had promised the owner of a chicken franchise to protect him in his right to exclude, to discriminate. As well, there were promises about who would be able to vote. Martin Luther King claimed that those promises constituted an unjust network. I think it is very instructive to look at just how he did so. He did so by asking the powerful people to change the rules, and the people whose opinion really matters, to meet with him. If they did, then he talked to them. He spoke on the premise that, "if you listen to me, you will come to the conclusion, as I have done, that your rules are wrong." He only engaged in civil disobedience when people refused to talk with him.

That's as far as I can go with an answer. I do believe that there is a justice with a capital "J." But it is impossible to discern with confidence. And so I am not too happy with natural rights or rights derived in any such way. I believe that there is, as I said, justice with a capital "J" out there, but we only discern it by engaging in critical conversation with one another. Here, the people, the oppressed, are very important. In raising their voices they make it possible for us to discover that our perception of what is just has actually been wrong.

DON SHAW, CHAIRMAN: Thank you Professor Heyne. Does that satisfy your question, sir...or your comment?

SPEAKER # 1: Yes, sir.

DON SHAW, CHAIRMAN: I see Mr. Justice Brownridge of the Saskatchewan Court of Appeal in the audience. I am not sure if he will want to make any comment or not.

We have another question.

SPEAKER #2: I find the comments of Ward Gasque and Dr. Paul Heyne somewhat ambiguous -- not really clear. Father Sadowsky, on the other hand, seems to have established that justice in property and aggression are inextricably bound together, and that clear thinking and clear definitions of those things are required to objectively deal with the problem and to come up with judgements which are just.

Ward Gasque in effect claimed that property is somehow granted by God and that people on earth are the stewards of this property. But, that doesn't really answer the question of how those individuals deal with property in our day-to-day transactions. How do they decide who owns what and to what purpose the property will be put? Similarly, Paul Heyne has talked about justice as something which is rather undefinable. It may be determined by consensus where people sit down and talk and come to some sort of democratic assessment of what it is. I wonder if those two gentlemen could define their positions a little more clearly, first on property and second on what justice is. How do you derive these concepts?

DON SHAW, CHAIRMAN: Do you have a preference as to the order? Would you like Dr. Gasque to define his concept of property?

SPEAKER #2: Yes, please.

DON SHAW, CHAIRMAN: ...and Dr. Heyne to define his concept of justice?

SPEAKER #2: Yes, please.

DON SHAW, CHAIRMAN: ...Thank you very much. Dr. Gasque...

WARD GASQUE: Maybe the reason that Father Sadowsky was clearer is that he happens to be a philosopher and we aren't. I'm certainly not a philosopher.

I suppose I would begin with the status quo and then take property as it exists, and as it would be defined in terms of our society -- ownership that we recognize. I would try to impress upon the individuals who have title to that property, in the broadest sense, their responsibilities to be stewards, to care for it, to use it for the common good, to use it for moral purposes, and so on. That's a very unsophisticated view, I suppose, but I would put the accent upon people who realize that there are many (perhaps theoretical) injustices.

I won't make injustice synonymous with inequality. All inequalities are not necessarily evil, but there may be many gross inequalities in our present situation. I would urge people to take them into consideration in trying to live morally, to use, to share, and to distribute the property that they have been entrusted with by God. That might have certain moral implications in terms of attitudes. Justice, from a theological perspective, is ultimately that which is in keeping with God's moral law.

- 17 -

Now, what happens if you're not a Christian? -- or a
Jew? -- and you don't accept the Old Testament tradition
about what God's moral law is? I don't interpret God's moral
law in an arbitrary sense. I think that God's moral law reflects
ultimate human values. It may be that all humans cannot
agree upon them, but they are not arbitrary. Therefore,
injustices are those things that go against this. In particular,
in the context of this discussion, they would be actions that
would infringe upon other people or hurt other people.

DON SHAW, CHAIRMAN: Thank you Dr. Gasque. Now, Dr.
Heyne.

PAUL HEYNE: I would say that...where is that gentleman?...
There you are.

I value clarity. But the approach I have learned to take
over the years to these questions is to use just as much clarity
as the situation requires, and no more. I once called it the
"Cartesian lust" -- the desire to have some perfectly clear
foundation. My friend Father Sadowsky exemplifies it. He
likes to build from a solid foundation and then deduce results.

I think that, in practice, this doesn't work. It doesn't
convince people. I much prefer the approach of the British
Common Law, which is also the common law of our countries,
Canada and the United States. I think it is a rich tradition.
The judges decide, with just as much clarity as they have to,
using whatever premises the contending parties will grant. I
think that is how we really settle serious questions and
disputes. We try to find out what the other party will grant
and that becomes our premise.

But we don't have to go back to define things if nobody is
asking for a definition. The pursuit of ultimate justification
lands us in an infinite regress anyway, so I would rather not go
back to those ultimate explanations. I would rather be
satisfied with just enough to convince you, or to convince the
parties who are contending. This approach also has the
advantage of not depending upon some absolute position. I am
saying, thereby, implicity, that I may be wrong, but I haven't
found out yet precisely where I may be wrong.

DON SHAW, CHAIRMAN: Thank you. Father Sadowsky, would like to say a word on that topic as well?

JAMES SADOWSKY: Of course, the Cartesian approach is convincing. If it can convince a person like me, there must be something right with it!

DON SHAW, CHAIRMAN: Thank you. We'll move on to the next question.

SPEAKER #3: I listened to Father Sadowsky with respect to his remarks regarding private property. I wish to make a comment. I would like to comment also on the introduction by Dr. Block when he talked about rent control. He said in effect that even the "left" is opposed to rent control. I got the impression that he was inferring that Gunnar Myrdal was opposed to rent control on the same grounds as the Fraser Institute is opposed to rent control. To leave this where it is would leave it out of context. It is true that Gunnar Myrdal is opposed to rent control, but only because he was in favour of a far more massive devotion of public funds to building housing to make rent reasonable. He saw that approach as making rent control unnecessary. But the Fraser Institute goes the other way and gives no indication of believing that public funds should furnish a basic minimum of rent at reasonable cost through the expenditure of public funds in the building of housing. I want to correct the impression that Gunnar Myrdal, if you read him correctly, came anywhere near the Fraser Institute approach of opposing rent control. Thank you.

DON SHAW, CHAIRMAN: Thank you sir. Since the comment was directed to Father Sadowsky's statement, would you care to respond to it, sir?

JAMES SADOWSKY: I am totally unfamiliar with this issue. I never heard the statement of Gunnar Myrdal until just now and I am thus in no position to comment.

SPEAKER #3: I was not asking a question. I was just offering a comment.

DON SHAW, CHAIRMAN: I realize that. Thank you. Do any other panelists wish to respond to this comment? No? In that case, we will go on to the next question.

SPEAKER #4: I am a professor in the School of Human Justice at the University of Regina. I would like to address my question to Paul Heyne. While we're on the subject of promises and obedience to the law and such things, one must remember "Patre san servander." I came here under the impression that we were going to be talking about theology, Third World development and economic justice. That is the broad rubric for this conference. However, you declined to address yourself to the South African situation. South Africa is part of the Third World and would seem to be a germane topic within which you could have discussed your thesis.

I would also like to ask why it is that you have confined yourself simply to the subject of rights and rules? When we talk about justice and the distribution of benefits and burdens we also use the criteria of need and desert. Yet you tended to gloss over those concepts. I think that in order to have a complete picture of how social systems distribute income and wealth one would need to play off in a coherent way needs, rights, and deserts, rather than maintain a rather partisan argument for one criterion only. So I would like to hear your comments on both of those points.

DON SHAW, CHAIRMAN: Thank you. Dr. Heyne?

PAUL HEYNE: There are other panels here and the other panels will deal with the Third World. I don't want to talk about South Africa, at least in my thesis, because I don't know enough about it. I would much rather talk about situations with which I am intimately familiar. I think that -- I know -- there are other panels. I don't think I am called upon to address all issues.

The other question is that of glossing over need and desert. I didn't intend to gloss them over. I talked very specifically about desert and I would say the same thing about need. The problem with these two criteria in large societies, by which I mean any society much beyond the family, is that we simply don't know what other people deserve or what other people need. What I was doing was rejecting need and desert as relevant criteria for policies in large societies.

DON SHAW, CHAIRMAN: Does that satisfy your question Professor? Thank you. Do either of the other panelists wish to comment? Let us take the next question.

SPEAKER #5: I'm a professor in the School of Human Justice at this University. I would also like to refer to the title of the panel which does raise, or is to raise, questions of economic justice, equality and Third World development. It seems to me we may be pussyfooting around the underlying question, which has to do with justice and inequality. While Professor Heyne has not, in this speech, mentioned his position on inequality and justice, there was a paper of his distributed for the closed conference prior to this one. In it he says, "Poverty is the consequence of low productivity, not of unequal distribution."

I would like to raise some questions about this view of inequality as somehow based on low productivity and not distribution. The approach to justice that is based on rules and laws completely sidesteps questions of power in the distribution of wealth. I would suggest that we could certainly consider Canada as a country which, in a relative sense, has had high productivity compared to the way most people in the world presently live, in terms of access to material circumstances. In Canada the bottom 20 per cent of the population earned 4 per cent of the income. The top 20 per cent of the population earned 42.5 per cent of the income. Perhaps a more telling statistic is that the bottom 60 per cent, in 1979 figures, earned less, 42 per cent, than the top 20 per cent, which earned 42.5 per cent. Now, my question: if inequality is not a result of...if poverty is not a result of unequal distribution of resources but of low productivity, how does Professor Heyne explain the distribution of income in this country and in most industrial countries, which has remained static through the last 30 or 40 years? And, as a second question, how can he sidestep issues of justice and poverty in view of that structural inequality of income?

DON SHAW, CHAIRMAN: Thank you, Professor. Are you clear on the question, Dr. Heyne?

PAUL HEYNE: I think I am. I take it that what you are doing is identifying or defining poverty as being at the bottom of some income distribution, without any regard to how high that income distribution is. Is that correct? That's what you seem to be saying....in fact, you even switched between inequality and poverty twice in your remarks. So, in other words, whoever is at the bottom 5 per cent of an income distribution would be, by your definition, poor -- right?

SPEAKER #5: Well, that is a debatable point. I think we can say...

PAUL HEYNE: ....I know, but you are assuming....

SPEAKER #5: I think that we can say that most native people would find themselves in that bottom 20 per cent, and that there is a number of indicators on mortality, housing, nutrition, incarceration rates, to indicate a very distinct relationship between their relatively low position and their access to material goods and quality of life.

PAUL HEYNE: ...right. Well, all I want to say is that when I talk about poverty I am thinking of it as measured by the criteria that you just mentioned. I am quite willing to grant that in the paper to which you refer I do mention that relative deprivation can also be defined legitimately as poverty. But I believe the quotation which you made was taken out of context. I don't recall exactly, but I think I was saying that poverty in most of the world throughout most of human history has been the result of low productivity. This, I think is a perfectly obvious statement. What I am saying is that throughout most of history, for most of the people in the world, redistribution of income within that society would not have eliminated poverty. That's all I was saying.

I don't know what else I ought to say in response to you. I'm certainly not trying to deny the existence of serious deprivation in Canada or the United States. I'm arguing that serious deprivation, suffering, what I will call absolute poverty, cannot be properly defined as being at the bottom of some income distribution. Yes, absolute poverty is a challenge -- a severe challenge -- an ethical challenge to the members of any affluent society, to any society which clearly has the resources to change that situation. And I am further saying that such poverty ought to be attacked justly.

DON SHAW, CHAIRMAN: Does either of the other panelists wish to comment on that question? Thank you. The next question.

SPEAKER #6: I am a grain farmer. I would like to make some comments in terms of my understanding of biblical justice. There seems a very fuzzy concept of justice being what people perceive justice to be. In my understanding, biblical justice would be determined by how well the society treats the poorest sector, or the least, or the weakest sector of society. That's the bias, as I understand it, of the Gospel. The Old Testament was always asking the question, "How well does the society take care of the people who happen to be in the weakest position to take care of themselves." So it's not a vague concept where one person's understanding of justice is equal to that of another. biblical justice is quite clearly an option on the side of the poor. And that's how you measure justice.

My second question is this. It really bothers me to hear it maintained that there is a clear distinction between the political and the economic aspects. My experience as a grain farmer is that the political and the economic factors are tied together, and that they are both tied to the concept of power. I see no reality in talking about a free exchange that's beneficial to everybody unless you address the question of power. I do not see how there is an equal exchange that benefits both people, when one person who is making an economic agreement is strong and powerful and the other person is weak and has no power.

DON SHAW, CHAIRMAN: Thank you. Dr. Heyne referred to the Constitution, and we haven't yet heard about the Crow rate or the National Energy Program! I am going to ask Dr. Gasque if he would respond to that comment.

WARD GASQUE: Yes, I'll respond to the first part in terms of biblical kinds of justice. I would say that that is certainly a central concern of the biblical prophets. But I think their concern for justice is broader than that. The prophets also talk about just weights, righteous relationships, and lying, whether it's between people at the highest level of the economic scale and the lowest, or people at the middle, or whatever. I wouldn't want to say that that is <u>the</u> only criterion, but it is certainly very important. We cannot judge a society without considering how it treats its weakest members. So, I would, with that qualification, agree with your comment.

I'm really not qualified to say much about the second part.

DON SHAW, CHAIRMAN: Would either of the other panelists care to comment on it?

JAMES SADOWSKY: Well, Rockefeller has to pay just as much for a haircut as I do, so I don't see how his superior wealth or power gives him any advantage as far as that transaction is concerned. I take it your point is that one's relative wealth enables him to profit more from an exchange than if he weren't rich. Is that the point you're making?

SPEAKER #6: That is certainly true of my own experience. It is true of my father, it is true of my grandfather. It is true of the way I understand the history of the prairies. Free exchange -- how much we get for our grain, what we pay for freight rates -- is an exchange between a powerful centralized group and thousands of individual farmers. It's not a fair agreement under those circumstances.

JAMES SADOWSKY: The question of power becomes relevant, it seems to me, if one of the parties forces the other to enter into the exchange. If the pressure to enter the exchange comes not from one of the parties but from the condition of the person himself, then I don't see any injustice in the exchange. If one person is making another an offer that he cannot resist, then I don't see how he is forcing an unwilling person to make the exchange. The necessity for making the exchange then arises out of the condition of the person himself, and I don't see an injustice there.

DON SHAW, CHAIRMAN: Thank you Father Sadowsky. As a grain farmer, of course, you come from one of the few markets that approaches the perfectly competitive model of economic theory.

The next question from this side, please.

SPEAKER #7: I am a representative of the Regina Council of Women. In the company of so many theologians and learned university scholars I must admit that I feel a little bit diffident standing here. However, I am compelled to speak. Dr. Gasque touched on the Old Testament laws of gleaning, sabbaticals, jubilee years, and Dr. Heyne mentions justice and rules. These rules apropos the poor have been laid down very clearly in the Old Testament and yet they have been forgotten, although I realize that universities do keep the sabbatical law. (Laughter)

DON SHAW, CHAIRMAN: Not without some controversy.

SPEAKER #7: I know Dr. Shaw.

Under those circumstances let us consider reverting to the Old Testament law. Then we have these rules. We have these methods of justice for distribution of wealth. When you lend somebody money, you take their coat as surety. If it gets cold at nighttime, you give them back their coat and take it back from them the following morning. This is just a minor rule, but it's there. And the gleanings -- once again the poor must be looked after. These rules are there. But churches, and the colonization of the Western world which has taken place by the Western countries as they have moved into the rest of the world, have completely forgotten all these rules. They produce the apartheid rules. They have produced the inequalities. I think that we have to look at where we are and how do we go back to the old rules. We have to start working within our own backyard, within the churches, and within the different religious orders. Because the rest of the world, for whom we are trying to do something, is not part of that religion. They have their own religions. It's our religions that have been pushed on them which have produced these inequalities.

DON SHAW, CHAIRMAN: You've raised an interesting question. Which of the panelists would care to start?

WARD GASQUE: I'd like to comment on that. When you raise the international dimension it gets more complex. In terms of our own Western societies, I would say we not only have not forgotten about those rules, they have had a tremendous influence on our society. The concept of graduated income tax, is an application, it seems to me, and an extension in a very significant way of some of these Old Testament laws. Our social welfare system is, it seems to me, an application of some of these Old Testament laws to a much more sophisticated society.

In terms of the 19th century, where charity was totally a private matter, people did go to the poor houses and children in Victorian England did run on the streets. That really has disappeared from our society because, I think, of the application of these ultimate principles. We have also been an extremely productive society in terms of economics, the way things have developed. This has enabled us to share the wealth in this sort of democratically agreed upon or socially agreed upon process. So, I think when you talk about the rest of the world it becomes much more complex. But in general principles, I believe that people in the West who have more should be concerned with sharing with people in other countries who have less. I'm not really an expert in international development but...I certainly favour encouraging the development of structures that would enable the Third World to attain standards of growth and wealth or betterment that we have had in our own Western societies. So, I think the influence of Christianity in the West has had a profound effect in actually meeting many of these needs. However, we have a long way to go.

DON SHAW, CHAIRMAN: Thank you. Does either of the other panelists wish to comment?

PAUL HEYNE: Just a quick comment on one small point. You stated that you represent the Reginal Council of Women, and spoke of the Old Testament rules. I think this ought to cause us to remember again that biblical injunctions and all other injunctions are not self-interpreting. I, for one, do not want to take the Old Testament rules on the status of women as normative for my society.

SPEAKER #7: Thank you, sir. The Regina Council of Women, is a large volunteer body and is carrying through the teachings of the Testaments to the best of its ability, being all volunteers and doing our best to....

PAUL HEYNE: ...with good judgement, I bet.

DON SHAW, CHAIRMAN: Thank you. Next question will come from this side.

SPEAKER #8: I'm a farmer. I would like to address the panel because I think there are some questions staring you in the face when you look at the women before you. It is an opportunity to test the beliefs and the theories that you have stated. I also am a Christian and I've traced, with excitement, through the Old Testament the understandings of the sabattic year, the year of jubilee, the time to study, to renew the land, to renew the people. And I have traced through what Jesus has done. The New Testament writings reveal that women for the first time are able to be addressed as human beings. And Jesus speaks with and addresses models of theology and philosophy with women and accords them an equal status which, although we spoke of the Genesis of God creating male and female in God's own image, we haven't honoured that to this point in time.

But now, through the Christian teachings we recognize that inequality, except that in our culture we can't find it. So I stand before you and ask the question of economics, of power, of speaking to the political power. How do we put those two things into practice when it comes to dealing with women in our society? It's trying to say, as Father Sadowsky says, that as long as you are not forced there is no problem. What happens, then, to women in our society who, in fact, are categorized differently or are paid less for work of equal value, or forced to work in factories? I say "forced" because economic force is also one that we need to recognize. So what do we do with those sorts of concrete things that stand before us in our society and test our theology?

DON SHAW, CHAIRMAN: Thank you. Father Sadowsky, would you care to respond to that?

JAMES SADOWSKY: Yes, it's a big question so I shan't be able to fully respond. If you have a free market, and you don't have restrictions on the employment of women, the tendency of the market is to pay women equally for the same work as men. To the extent that the work is equal, they do tend to get paid the same salary. Consider the following: if you have two groups of equally productive people, one insisting on working for a higher salary than the other, those who insist on the higher salary would be fired. So ultimately the salaries do become equal. Our big problem is not the fact that women are not getting equal pay for equal work, it is rather that women are in lower-paying jobs than men, although the payment for those jobs is equal. That seems to be the real problem. Why does that happen? I think it happens basically because of the choice in lifestyle of women. Perhaps for cultural reasons, women choose to enter into arrangements like marriage and childbearing that make it difficult for them to go into these better paying jobs. If women behaved more like men then they would probably have the same kinds of jobs as men.

DON SHAW, CHAIRMAN: Thank you, Father Sadowsky.

SPEAKER #8: I have two responses to that. One is, where are we to find that society where women are always paid the same as men? And two, at what point are men going to start raising the children or start having the children?

WARD GASQUE: Could I make a comment? I would just like to say that on biblical as well as moral grounds I would affirm equality of male and female. I would personally fight against any attempt to discriminate against women economically and I therefore think Father Sadowsky's answer is a bit limited. (Laughter) I am aware from my own observations of a significant number of places where women really are paid less for doing essentially the same job as men. I support laws against this, and I will apply whatever political pressures I have in society to resist this, to fight against it, and to speak out against it as a clear injustice. I strongly affirm women's roles as equal to those of men in society. They must be given the same opportunities and be paid the same as anyone else.

DON SHAW, CHAIRMAN: Thank you. You have raised an interesting issue. Dr. Heyne now wishes to comment on it.

PAUL HEYNE: I have two brief comments. They may not settle anything but here goes. Statistical averages on relative wages of men and women conceal a lot of things. They should therefore be used carefully. One of the reasons that women's average salaries as a percentage of men's haven't been going up in recent years is because so many more women are entering the labour force. Naturally, they tend to enter at low-salaried levels, and that brings the average down. I think this is true in Canada, and I know it's true in the United States. In contrast, men are tending to leave the labour force, mainly from the low wage sectors. And that tends to bring the average male wage up. So you have to be careful.

Now my second observation. Recently, a lot of studies have shown, at least in North American culture, perhaps in Western European culture, (I'm not sure about that), that women demonstrate in all sorts of empirical ways a greater interest in the welfare of children. This seems to be a fact, and as long as that is a fact women are going to be more likely to quit their jobs. I don't know why that's a factor. Certainly I am not going to say it's based on biology, but there are all sorts of studies that show when sacrifices have to be made...well, the simple fact is that men desert their families...that women just are more willing to make sacrifices. They seem to be more interested in the welfare of children. Now that's going to affect their job chances and wages.

Then there's a third quick observation. This relates to justice. In Seattle we have a law which says that contracting firms owned by women have to be given a certain percentage of all city jobs. That's because women contractors were discriminated against by the city in the past. Now, this is true. Women contractors were discriminated against by the city in the past. But the women contractors who are now getting special treatment are the daughters of the men who were the contractors in the last generation -- the ones who received the privileges. This is an interesting example of how the pursuit of justice often entails more injustice.

DON SHAW, CHAIRMAN: Thank you. We'll take the next question.

SPEAKER #9: I teach in the Psychology Department here at the University. I have a question to address to each of the panel members regarding Dr. Block's opening remarks where he defined the task of the Fraser Institute in sharing esoteric economic knowledge with the Canadian people. Were you a participant at the recent invitation-only session which the Fraser Institute just concluded? And if you were, who were the other people there?

WARD GASQUE: Yes, I was a participant.

PAUL HEYNE: Yes, I was too. I don't think the membership is a secret. I am puzzled by that question.

SPEAKER #9: Would you mind telling us who the other participants were, especially the people from the local scene?

PAUL HEYNE: I don't think that it's my function to answer that.

SPEAKER #9: Do you believe that the purpose of the Fraser Institute is to share esoteric economic knowledge with the Canadian people?

PAUL HEYNE: The purpose of the conference that I attended was for people to talk with one another, to exchange ideas. We weren't trying to disseminate any information outside.

SPEAKER #9: So your answer is, on this question, you refuse to dialogue.

PAUL HEYNE: No, I am saying I do not think it is my function to answer the question. I don't remember their names. I met most of them for the first time.

DON SHAW, CHAIRMAN: Father Sadowsky, do you have a response?

JAMES SADOWSKY: I was a participant and I don't know who most of the people were.

WALTER BLOCK: Can I take the microphone for a second? Is it all right if I speak, sir?

DON SHAW, CHAIRMAN: Very briefly, Walter.

WALTER BLOCK: I have never been asked for the names of the people in the previous session until this gentleman did. This is a matter of public knowledge, as far as I am concerned. If the gentleman will see me later I will furnish him with a list, as I would have, had anyone else asked me.

DON SHAW, CHAIRMAN: You are quite prepared to provide the list of participants?

WALTER BLOCK: Sure.

DON SHAW, CHAIRMAN: Thank you. (Scattered applause.)
The next question from this side.

SPEAKER #10: Many of the questions I would have liked to ask have already been raised. I would like to comment on some of the answers. I am a concerned citizen. I'm actually a landed immigrant. I'm a peace activist and homemaker.

I think it is very difficult to make blanket statements about women's interest in children, whether they are more interested in children than men are, when there are all kinds of factors that you are not really looking at. It might be that women stay out of the work force and remain at home and look after their children. One reason for this might be that they haven't got a snowball's chance in Hell of making as much money going out to work as their husbands. If the husband stays at home and looks after the children and the wife goes out to work instead, that's one thing. But everyone doesn't have equal access to contraception, and women do not have easy access to abortion. They are forced into bearing children whether they want to or not. Day care is not provided in sufficient quantities or quality to provide a reasonable alternative.

DON SHAW, CHAIRMAN: The topic is Religion, Egalitarianism and Economic Justice. Presumably, at the moment, in my interpretation, we are speaking of economic justice.

SPEAKER #10: I think we are absolutely on the point, thank you.

DON SHAW, CHAIRMAN: Well, that comes in the next panel.

SPAKER #10: Well, maybe one of the panelists would comment on that?

DON SHAW, CHAIRMAN: All right, thank you. Which panelist would like to comment briefly on that?

SPEAKER #10: It should be Paul Heyne. Also, I should like to know what he thinks about the fact that American women couldn't get the Equal Rights Amendment passed last year?

PAUL HEYNE: Well, I was referring to a substantial body of literature in sociology, psychology, and other disciplines. It may not be persuasive, but it certainly strongly suggests that women in North America, for whatever reasons, are more committed to the welfare of children. They are more concerned about the welfare of children. I would tell you where you could find that literature....I'm not evaluating it...I....

SPEAKER #10: I'm suggesting that we have got incomplete evidence when we don't actually have an experimental situation where women are given a real choice.

PAUL HEYNE: This might be a fault of the literature. But some of it utilizes very sophisticated statistical techniques to try to control for other variables. Much of the literature is cited in the notes and bibliography of a book by Victor Fuchs. It is entitled How We Live and it's a description of American experience. But much of it would be relevant to Canadian life too. You would find the sources in there.

DON SHAW, CHAIRMAN: Perhaps the speaker and Dr. Heyne could discuss this during the coffee break that comes up in a few minutes.

SPEAKER #10: OK. I think it's pretty evident to everyone how well women are represented on the panel.

(Scattered applause.)

DON SHAW, CHAIRMAN: I might say it's not for lack of women having been invited.

Let us now take the next question. I think we will probably have room for two more questions before the break.

SPEAKER #11: I'm here because I'm interested in any forum that discusses Third World economic development. I would like the panelists to relate their different views on the third world situation. We haven't yet heard that. I would like that to be done in a few sentences, if possible. And also, since they are talking about poverty, and economic justice, let me relate my experience of it.

From the age of six I have been brought up by the Catholic church. And my experience with the church and with those responsible for running it, is that economic justice, that is supposed to be applicable to everybody, is non-existent. For instance, in my village, when everybody lived in mud houses, the priests and the religious people lived in mansions that were constructed out of the people's labour and out of the people's low income. And they also built humungous churches. You know, the church in my village is more important than you can imagine. It is so beautiful. And it is constructed from the people's labour and the payments they have made. When I went home recently the same situation was still there.

DON SHAW, CHAIRMAN: Pardon me for interrupting, please. Does your question relate specifically to Third World development?

SPEAKER #11: Well, yes.

DON SHAW, CHAIRMAN: If it does, would it inconvenience you to defer it until the next panel which deals with that topic specifically?

SPEAKER #11: What is the primary discussion?

DON SHAW, CHAIRMAN: The order of the presentation of the panels has been changed. This panel deals with economic justice and egalitariansim, not specifically with Third World development.

SPEAKER #11: Yes, but the whole topic is on Third World development. I would like the members of <u>this</u> panel to give us their views on it.

DON SHAW, CHAIRMAN: I really do think that if the question relates specifically to Third World development, it would more appropriately be made at the next panel. Well, if it relates to economic justice, what is your question, sir?

SPEAKER #11: It is this. How do the promises of the Bible relate to the economic situation in the Third World?

DON SHAW, CHAIRMAN: To whom do you wish to address the question?

SPEAKER #11: Any of the panelists.

DON SHAW, CHAIRMAN: Which panelist would wish answer the question?

JAMES SADOWSKY: Well, I am not an expert on Third World development. I am a theologian and I do have friends who come from the Third World who are believing Christians. I have North American friends who live and work in the third world. I would say one thing. I think there has been some evidence to suggest that the acceptance of Christianity does give people a different attitude towards their own world and their relationship to Creation. My little contribution as a theologian is to encourage the proclamation of the Gospel. This can be seen, for example, in Latin America, in the growth of the Pentecostal Protestant churches. And in Africa, with the growth of the indigenous independent churches, there has been a tremendous correlation between the indigenization of Christianity with actual economic self-development and progress. That is not all the answer, but in terms of my own sphere of influence that is one thing I'm involved in.

DON SHAW, CHAIRMAN: Thank you. We have run out of time on this panel. I will accept one more question and I ask further questioners or commentators to defer their questions until one of the later panels. Yes, sir.

SPEAKER #12: I'm a farmer and I am going to make it very short. My question is, when will Christ return? How soon will He return to earth and where? And when He does return to earth, wherever it may be, where is He going to set his peak next on the earth? What place? If anyone would be able to answer me?

DON SHAW, CHAIRMAN: It's a short question. I'm not sure the answer can be short. (Laughter)

WARD GASQUE: I'll attempt to answer that. Jesus said no one knows the day and hour, not even the Son of God himself, and therefore I am sure that no one on the panel knows the answer to that question. (laughter)

PAUL HEYNE: No, but I would also like to say, if I may, that I think Christians are called to realize the Kingdom of God in preparation for that. I believe that that is not exactly done by churches. Someone said that Jesus came from claiming the Kingdom of God but what he got was the church.

DON SHAW, CHAIRMAN: Ladies and gentlemen, I thank the panelists very much for their discussion and I thank members of the audience very much for their participation.

PANEL # 2

LIBERATION THEOLOGY
AND THIRD WORLD DEVELOPMENT

LORD PETER BAUER

BERNARD ZAGORIN, CHAIRMAN: Welcome to our discussion on Liberation Theology and Third World Development. Because of time constraints and because one of our panel members has to leave to catch a plane, I am anxious to get started. I call to your attention that there is a dinner break from 5:15 to 7:00 p.m. a dinner break and after that, the last panel, Ethical Reflections on the Economic Crisis will take place from 7:00 to 8:30 p.m., so that we have a lot of ground to cover yet.

We have three panel members. I want to introduce now Professor Peter Bauer, who has been for over 20 years a Professor of Economics at the London School of Economics. Professor Bauer, the floor is yours.

PETER BAUER: (applause) I propose to discuss official foreign aid, that is, government-to-government wealth transfers from the West to Third World governments. This is a policy much favoured by Liberation Theologians. In fact, it is in the forefront of their proposals.

The principal argument behind this policy has always been that it is necesary for the development of the Third World and the relief of poverty there. In fact, foreign aid is much more likely to obstruct than to promote these objectives. I want to begin by first quoting two examples of the central argument for this policy both from prominent sources, one dating from 1961, the other from 1981. In 1961 Professor Paul Samuelson, Nobel Laureate, wrote in his celebrated text book, "Backward nations cannot get their heads above water because their production is so low that they can spare nothing for capital formation by which their standard of living could be raised." In 1981, Professor Hollis Chenery of Harvard, formerly Vice-President in charge of economic research at the World Bank, said, "Foreign aid is a central component of world development."

These assertions are altogether divorced from reality. If Professor Samuelson were right, how could innumerable individuals, groups, societies and countries have emerged from poverty to prosperity without external donations, as they have done the world over? And how could foreign aid be the central component of world development when so much development has taken place, and still takes place, without foreign aid? The capital demands for development, so far from being a crucial obstacle to Third World progress, are a non-problem. Where the required personal, cultural, social and political conditions are present, capital will be generated locally, or provided from abroad commercially. People who can use capital productively will either generate it themselves or secure it from others. Thus, in the Third World, governments or businesses which can use capital productively can borrow at home and abroad. The volume of investable funds is not a critical determinant of economic improvement. If it were, large numbers of very poor people could not have attained prosperity in the space of a few years as they have done the world over -- as for instance, the immigrant communities in North America and Southeast Asia. There are countless other examples.

Third World Progress

Still less is foreign aid necessary for progress in the Third World any more than it was necessary for the development in the West. Large parts of the Third World made rapid progress long before foreign aid was invented. Witness Southeast Asia, West Africa, Latin America, which were practically transformed in the century before the 1950s, long before the advent of foreign aid. Emergence of hundreds of millions of people, both in the South and in the West, from poverty to prosperity has not depended on external gifts. Economic achievement has depended and still does depend on people's own faculties, motivations, and mores, their institutions and the policies of their rulers. In short, economic achievement depends on the conduct of people, including governments.

As Third World governments and businesses which can use capital effectively can borrow commercially abroad, it follows that the maximum contribution of official aid to development is the cost of borrowing that is avoided, as a percentage of the national income. The maximum possible contribution of aid to development must, therefore, be quite small. Nevertheless, aid which cannot do much good for development can do much harm. This sounds paradoxical because aid represents a gift of resources. The paradox is resolved when it is recognized that aid, unlike manna from heaven, can have adverse repercussions. These repercussions affect the basic personal, social and political determinants of economic development. The expectations set up by the amounts of aid, which were not modest relative to the national income of the recipients, may be significant, and often are significant, relative to other magnitudes, especially to government revenues and foreign exchange receipts. And these are the relevant magnitudes because foreign aid, official aid, accrues to government. Government aid as a proportion of government revenues and export earnings aid must be higher and is usually many times greater than it is a percentage of the national income.

Now, let me turn to some of the adverse repercussions. To begin with, aid greatly increases resources at the disposal of the recipient government. This has inevitably reinforced the politicization in life in the Third World, increased the prizes of political power, and the intensity of stuggle for it. It has exacerbated stress and conflict, especially in multi-racial and multi-cultural societies. Much energy, ingenuity and effort have been applied either to acquire power or a share in it, or else to avoid the consequences of it exercised by others.

Government Intervention

It has also much enhanced the abilities of government to implement policies detrimental to living standards and material progress. Examples include under-payment of farmers, which discourages the output of food and export crops and emergence from subsistance production. As well, there is forced collectivization, and suppression of trading activities. This has aggravated the effect of crop failure in famine areas in Africa. Then, too, there is discrimination against productive minorities and their harrassment, or worse. Witness for instance, the Asians in East Africa. To this list must be added subsidization of uneconomic manufacturing activity.

Relief of poverty is the other most widely advertised benefit of official aid. We have seen that it cannot achieve this, nor promote development. In fact, harmful policies buttressed by aid usually damage the poorest, most notably the rural poor. This is the result of the urban bias of Third World economic policies. Aid goes to government, that is, to the ruler, not to the pitiable figures familiar in aid publicity. To give money to Third World governments on the ground that most of their subjects are poor, differs completely from giving money to the poor themselves. The policies of aid-recipient governments, including their patterns of public spending, are rarely governed by the needs of the very poor. How is it that the very poor in Pakistan, Tanzania, Malawi or Nigeria benefit from the creation, at vast expense, of new capital cities? Many bizarre anomalies result from giving money to the rulers on the basis of the poverty of their subjects regardless both of the policies pursued, and of general living conditions. I mention here only one.

If a government expels its most productive citizens, for instance ethnic minorities, with incomes above the national average, then on the basis of poverty it can claim more aid because incomes are now lower!

Besides the promotion of development and the relief of poverty in the Third World, many subsidiary and ad hoc arguments have emerged in the advocacy of aid ranging from redress for alleged Western mis-deeds to the rescue of Western banks. I must conclude my talk at this point, but I shall be happy to answer questions about these and other issues of economic development.

BERNARD ZAGORIN, CHAIRMAN: Thank you Professor Bauer.

LIBERATION THEOLOGY
AND THIRD WORLD DEVELOPMENT

DR. MURDITH MacLEAN

BERNARD ZAGORIN, CHAIRMAN: Our next speaker is Dr. Murdith MacLean, a Professor of Philosophy at St. John's College, the University of Manitoba. Dr. MacLean.

MURDITH MacLEAN: Thank you.

I was going to begin by saying that everyone thinks foreign aid is at least a good thing to those less well-off than ourselves. It may appear that we have at least one disagreement on that contention in the panel. But I want to begin with the generalization that I think most of us do believe that we should at least attempt to do what we can, to some extent, to benefit those who are less well off than we are.

Where we differ, I think, is on how urgent that is -- whether it is something, for instance, that is not only admirable but our duty. If it is, how ought we to go about doing it? Should it be a matter of taxation and political redistribution, or something that is strictly left up to the voluntary goodwill of the population?

I am not going to try and answer all those sorts of questions. Instead I shall try to provide a very rough sketch of what I think is crucial in understanding the Christian contribution to this kind of issue. I am going to try and sketch something of what I think is a quite deeply-rooted element in the Christian world-view. It is only one part of the picture and I don't want to suggest for a minute that only Christians take this stance, but certainly Christians do.

First of all, the Christian world-view is, from the beginning, and from all its inheritance, intensely corporate. From the Old Testament and right through the New we do not see human kind merely as a bunch of individuals. We see it as a family, an inter-related and inter-dependent family, of brothers and sisters, together in the family of God. God's covenant was with Israel, not with individual Israelites. What was saved was the new Israel, the church, not just a group of individuals. That is an important starting point.

Second, the earth is the Lord's and the fullness thereof, say the Psalms (and it is equally a part of the Jewish and the Christian tradition) that God has lent it to this people; the human kind of which I spoke earlier, as a family together. And what is equally clear from the Old Testament tradition is that in giving the world to a people, God doesn't just give the rocks and the trees and the uncultivated fields, but also the things that the earth produces when its people use it.

Theistic Outlook

What I would like to stress is that when you engage in a dialogue between those who have this kind of outlook, let's call it a theistic outlook, and those who don't, it's not just that we agree about what the world is like but disagree on whether there is an additional inhabitant in it, God. Rather, it is that everything is different, the whole picture is different, and I am trying to sketch the way in which it is so. For from those differences in viewpoint follow some differences in the way in which you treat what you have in front of you.

It follows from what I have said, very crudely and very roughly, that we may no longer see the other individuals in this world merely as individuals that we have happened to be born next to. We are together members of the family. We are inter-dependent. One consequence of that, to put it in something like the jargon of moral philosophy, is that we can no longer think of our duties as limited to refraining from injuring other people. We have more than just the duty to refrain from committing injustices. It follows from this theistic view of things whereby we are members together of a family, and we share in common the world and its resources, that those are things which we have a duty to share with one another. So we have positive duties as Christians to share. It's not just an optional extra.

Sharing in Common

Now, what does this imply for the primary motive of a Christian, and for other theists who hold this view of sharing the world's goods? It implies that we not think only that unequal distribution arises from mal-use of the world's resources and from oppression; though it might, in many cases, but that is not the motivation anyway. The motivation is simply that these are goods we share in common. And while my brother or my sister is less well off than I am, I owe a share of it to him or her. Now, there are lots of things that need to be specified further, including the circumstances in which we do the sharing and how we devise it. But, I think that is where we must start.

There is a problem with all this, however. What do I do if I hold this theistic view and I hold it in a pluralistic society? I can well imagine other persons in the society saying, "Well that's just great. I'm glad you theists hold that view, especially if I turn out some day to be less well off. But I don't hold that view. And in my opinion, it's a good thing, it's a noble thing, it's a fine thing to share the wealth if you choose to do that. But it's not something I think you ought to oblige me to do. Not something, for instance, you ought to tax me to do in order that you might share the proceeds with the inhabitants of other countries."

I think it is morally right to tax Canadians for the purpose of sharing with the less fortunate. And the reason I think it's right is that it is right for us, those of us who share this view, to try and convince the nations of which we are members, that that is a proper view of humankind and the proper response to this view of humankind. I don't believe it's right to do it by fiat. I think it is right to do it as a result of a political process in which we convince one another in the rightness of this way of seeing things, and this way of doing things.

Distribution Techniques

I don't think it follows from this view for a moment that the techniques of distribution, that the means by which we bring aid, are crystal clear right from the beginning. They're not. And we may have to attend very clearly and carefully to the advice we get from the social scientists, from the economists regarding what things actually do bring aid. It's hard for me to share all of Professor Bauer's view of what does bring aid, but I must confess that in that area I am quite ignorant. And it is also quite clear that we are going to have to ask the advice of those who know more about this than philosophers are apt to know. What really does benefit those people we are attempting to aid? I'm pretty sure, though I can't afford to be absolutely sure about this either, that what we thought of so far in terms of foreign aid is not the only sort of thing that we could think of as foreign aid.

One last comment. Even if the Christian moral analysis is true, we must still listen to the advice of the social scientists as to what things really do assist our neighbours, our brothers and sisters. It may well also be the case that as a result of this different picture of things, this different world-view, we look in different places for evidence. It may be that when we look there we see different things as being right or wrong in comparison with the person who doesn't share this world-view. I think this is where some of the outcries from those who have the feelings of the oppressed have arisen.

BERNARD ZAGORIN: Thank you Dr. MacLean.

LIBERATION THEOLOGY
AND THIRD WORLD DEVELOPMENT

PROFESSOR RICK HORDERN

BERNARD ZAGORIN: Our next speaker is Dr. Hordern who is a Professor of Religious Studies at Luther College. His doctoral dissertation was written in the area of Liberation Theology. Dr. Hordern.

RICK HORDERN: Liberation Theology has emerged in many parts of the world. I especially want to focus on Latin America and Liberation Theology there because that is where, I think, the question of economic development can best be highlighted. I assume that most of us here are aware of the severe forms of poverty affecting many parts of Latin America today. It is estimated that over 90 per cent of Latin Americans are living in poverty and endure various levels of malnutrition and disease.

But there is a dimension to Latin American poverty of which I know that not all are aware -- namely, that this poverty has increased and become much worse in recent decades. For centuries, the Latin American economy has been centred around the small elite which owns most of the land. The majority of population worked for the land owners. A generation ago this began to change. Advanced technology and mechanization were introduced into farming with the result that people who worked the land suddenly found themselves unemployed. They were left with no land to live on, or on which to raise food for themselves. At the same time the industrialized nations, and especially the United States, decided that the economic cure for Latin America would be found in promoting the industrialization of the economy. In countries like Brazil, much investment from trans-national corporations was rapidly made in the cities. With the need now for urban workers, many of the farmers who were evicted from their land went to the cities in search of employment. Unfortunately the process of industrialization did not even begin to produce the number of jobs needed. Only some people benefited. And thus urban poverty began to flourish. Likewise, the debt taken on by the host countries to entice investment has now become unpayable, and many countries will live in perpetual debt to the advanced nations.

Another problem has been the rise of military dictatorships and the industrial police state to control economic development.

One Crop Farming

As well, there has been the emergence of the cash crop. Historically, many countries had been self-sufficient in producing their own food. But then the land owners converted their agricultural holdings into raising one particular crop for export sales. The feeling was that the income from foreign sales would make possible the purchase of needed food from overseas. But the strategy has not worked. Fluctuating international markets frequently robbed the crop of its profitablity. In some parts of the world, the specialized farming has proven unadaptable to local climate. The net result, all too often, has been a shortage of money to purchase food from overseas. This means that the local population which had been adequately nourished before, now faces hunger and malnutrition. The net result of these factors has been increased poverty on a scale never before experienced in Latin America. And these forces have also hurt people in other parts of the world.

Liberation Theology emerged in Latin America in light of the poverty and injustices faced by the populace. An increasing number of church people found themselves working actively for fundamental changes in the structures of their nations. Liberation Theology emerged in light of this quest for liberation from the political, economic, social and spiritual forces which were dehumanizing the population. Liberation theology seeks then to reflect on God and the church in light of this committment to liberation. I think it is important to note that Liberation Theology does not seek to bring about a "Christain society." The movement for liberation and freedom, including economic justice, is seen as a project in which both Christians and non-Christians are active. In this sense there is no Christian blueprint for a liberated social order.

Social Justice

The primary concern of the church is not to debate whether to support capitalism or socialism. The primary concern is how to help people who are in need, who are being exploited in an unjust situation. The mainline churches have always affirmed that among the functions ordained by God for political government is the call to promote justice for all people. For example, in the Lutheran heritage it was Martin Luther who called upon local governments to raise money through taxation that would be used for the relief of the poor. In the Roman Catholic tradition, it was Pope Leo XIII who made it clear that all actions of the church for social relief had to be based on social justice. In other words, individual works of charity are not a substitute for social justice. Rather, they must supplement justice.

Thus, we can see how the Latin American Liberation Theology is part of this on-going Christian tradition. Now it is true that while Liberation Theology upholds no specific political or economic system as intrinsically ideal, most of its support is toward some form of socialism. Free enterprise capitalism has been one of the major villains in producing unemployment and poverty, and so they are looking for alternative models. Liberation theologians are seeking neither capitalism nor socialism nor communism, but rather a form of economy suited to their own context which will enhance the liberation of the people. It is not fair to equate Liberation Theology with Marxism. However, many Latin American theologians have a high regard for Marxist social analysis as a way of analyzing current poverty, and as a way of putting together strategies for a more just future.

Marxism

The basic difference, of course, between Christianity and Marxism, would lie in the Marxist view of dialectical materialism and its related atheism. However, in Latin America, the philosophical differences are secondary, because so often Christians and Marxists have found themselves working side by side on common social objectives. As the Latin American community continues its quest for alternative economic systems, we should also note that the Christian tradition has always upheld a special sympathy for economic attitudes that would lend more support to a socialist kind of option. For example, Christians regard material wealth as a blessing from God that is intended to be shared with others. In contrast, capitalism tends to regard wealth as the individual's natural reward for work or investment. Christians have generally affirmed that one should be satisfied with the standard of living that meets one's basic needs to enjoy life. But the accumulation of surplus wealth is wrong. And yet capitalism is based on the assumption that people will seek to accumulate additional capital. Christians have always opposed greed and selfishness -- which all too often are the basic motivating factors in the capitalist system. By contrast, socialism, at least in theory, strives to encourage productivity by appealing to a vision of a better life for all.

However, in all fairness, we must note that present-day socialist societies have not always been successful on the matter of productivity. While reasons for Christians interest in socialism are evident, it must be added that there is not by any means an uncritical acceptance of socialism among church leaders. Current socialist systems evidence a number of problems. All too often we find, as in capitalism, an exaggerated emphasis on economic performance fueling a rampant materialism and creating a blindness toward racism, sexism, and other human rights violations. Nor are socialist states always in the vanguard of protecting religious liberty and other forms of human freedom. In principle, Christians are unwilling to sacrifice religious freedom for economic security just as they are unwilling to sacrifice social justice in the name of freedom. But, of course, we would have to define the word "freedom" more carefully. For example, it does not mean the absolute right of the individual; nor can we define freedom without considering who it is that has power.

The Christian knows that the present order was fashioned by human beings. It is not the way God intended things to be and there is both human responsibility for social justice plus the potential that human beings can rectify the situation. The Bible gives us a vision of the world based on justice and peace and it is that vision which constantly calls us to seek ways of creating a better future.

Thank you.

BERNARD ZAGORIN, CHAIRMAN: Thank you Professor Hordern.

LIBERATION THEOLOGY
AND THIRD WORLD DEVELOPMENT

DISCUSSION

BERNARD ZAGORIN, CHAIRMAN: May I remind you ladies and gentlemen about the guidelines for questions or comments. In order to allow more people to ask questions, or to make comments to the panelists, may I suggest they be short and sweet. The question should be put to a specific member, or to the panel in general. Each panelist always has the right to make a comment even though not specifically addressed. This procedure will give more people time to speak on these very interesting issues.

    Yes, sir, you first.

SPEAKER #13: I work on development issues in Regina. In some sense I agree with panelist Lord Bauer concerning the effect of aid on poverty. However, I would like to turn this around a bit. In one country in the Caribbean where I've lived, the effect of aid was to create a dam that flooded a whole farming area. This put people off the land, destroyed the self-sufficiency of rice for that country, and created cheap labour for free trade zones that export baseballs to the United States. Now that's the effect of aid...a Western aid and a Western strategy of free trade zones, which I understand some people here really support. That is an example of an ill-conceived aid program.

    But there are three types of aid. There is bilateral, multilateral and non-governmental aid. This latter is people-centred development, where the aid is received by the people who need it, where it really helps people, where the aid meets the people's concerns. As someone who has worked with that sort of development I would like to defend it.

BERNARD ZAGORIN, CHAIRMAN: Can we keep the speech short though? If it's going to be a talk....

SPEAKER #13: ...just a dialogue. (laughter) I would like to dialogue with one of the panelists and ask a question of Lord Bauer. I would like to support what Professor MacLean was saying, however. I would like to point out that when you ask what good development is, the best people to talk to are the people in the developing countries themselves; that is, the people in the villages, in the communities of the Third World. That is what private aid does. So I would like to ask Lord Bauer this. Is he making a blanket condemnation of aid, that is, all aid from the West? Or is he just referring to the misconceived aid that governments give, as in my first example? Thank you.

LORD BAUER: Let me clarify matters. I spoke only of government-to-government wealth transfer known as aid. I did not address myself to the question of the work of voluntary agencies. Because I believe that the relief of poverty is an accute need, it is a task for voluntary agencies, preferably non-politicized charities. I think the use of the term "aid" has been most unfortunate because the use of the term has three effects simultaneously. It disarms all criticism, it prejudges results and it obscures the reality of the policy. Nobody can be against aid to the less fortunate. It has encouraged an uncritical axiomatic approach to the whole question of assessing aid. As a policy we really must look at what are the repercussions at the recipient end. This is a very complex question but I firmly come down on the side of voluntary agencies as distinct from government-to-government trans-fers.

BERNARD ZAGORIN, CHAIRMAN: Thank you. Over here, please.

SPEAKER #14: Thank you for the opportunity. I think we must address economic injustice directly. We must ask why exploitation is allowed in the world to the extent where it is destroying our very freedom. I would like to point out that the reason for the failure to achieve economic justice is that exploitation, rather than honesty, is favoured. And here is where it starts. Those who would wish to capture and hold the supreme power have got it in their hands by not monetizing real wealth honestly and forcing borrowed money in its place. This is what causes unemployment. This is what causes non-productivity or poor productivity in general. During World War II we had economic justice on the Allied side at least where we priced agricultural materials in balance with all other sectors of the economy. I have with me some facts, some statistics to prove that is the proper direction to go.

Since 1952 we scrapped parity pricing for agriculture and substituted it with borrowed income rather than earned income. At the present time this is the cause of economic injustice.

BERNARD ZAGORIN, CHAIRMAN: Excuse me, sir. Could I ask you to whom this is directed? If it is directed to someone in particular, could you make it shorter so that other people might also have the chance to speak.

SPEAKER #14: Well, I think the gentleman on your right would be the one to whom I would address it. If it be your wish I could quote a few of the statistical facts that I have with me. If not, I'll leave them out.

BERNARD ZAGORIN, CHAIRMAN: I think it would be better to leave those out for the time being and give Professor Bauer a chance to respond.

LORD BAUER: If I understood the question correctly, like many other people this gentleman equates economic injustice with wide income differences. I believe that income differences can never be discussed sensibly except by looking at the background. It is by no means necessary that even very wide income differences reflect exploitation. Let me give you three examples.

In Hindu society and in South Asia generally, people object to taking animal life. For example, many societies never kill cattle. It is not surprising that people who take such attitudes (and indeed it has become an integral part of their spiritual lives) should be materially less well off than those who do not impose such restraints on themselves.

Second, in Islamic countries, women are discouraged from working outside the home. That immediately greatly reduces per capita income compared to other countries where there are no such restrictions.

In Southeast Asia the richest people by far are Chinese traders, merchant ship operators, mine owners, plantation owners who came in as penniless coolies. It is not surprising that they should be much better off materially than others who are less ambitious.

I think the way to look at income differences is this. Originally, everybody is poor. Some people have emerged from this poverty sooner and to a greater extent than have others. But these differences do not mean that those who are better off, that is, earlier emergers, have obstructed the emergence of others. On the contrary, the newly rich can tow others along. There are exceptions to this phenomenon, but there are not many.

BERNARD ZAGORIN, CHAIRMAN: Thank you. Professor MacLean.

MURDITH MacLEAN: I would like to agree with Professor Bauer but add a word, I think, that pulls in another direction as well. I think he is absolutely right to say that you can't always tell from a difference in income level that there is some injustice involved. Certainly you can't tell that there has always been exploitation. But I also think it is right to say that where there is a difference in income, there is a prima facie case for saying it should be explained. There should be an explanation of why the differential exists, and only some explanations will justify it. And there are many explanations which we now accept as justifying income differences and differences in wealth which we ought not to accept.

BERNARD ZAGORIN, CHAIRMAN: Thank you.
    This gentleman over here.

SPEAKER #15: I've a question or two for Professor Bauer. They are based upon his paper that was delivered recently, "Ecclesiastical Economics: Envy Legitimized." And my questions are addressed as well to what you've just said a moment ago. In your paper you state, and I quote, "One of the prime reasons for poverty of the poor has nothing to do with the lack of natural resources, including land. It has little or nothing to do with the poverty of individuals or societies. In the less-developed world today many millions of extremely poor people have abundant cultivatable land. Over much of Asia, Africa, Latin America, very large numbers of extremely poor and backward people live in areas where cultivatable but uncultivated land is free or extremely cheap. The small size and low productivity of the farms in the presence of landless workers in such areas reflect not the shortage of land, but primarily the lack of ambition, enterprise and skill."

Now, I don't know what newspapers you have been reading. I don't know what countries you have been visiting. But I find this description of the land tenure systems, for example, in Latin America, so far out of touch with reality that I really wonder what it is you are describing. These facts are empirically incorrect. We are now witnessing and have witnessed historically in Latin America the complete destruction of indiginous populations with their own land tenure systems. We are now witnessing the slaughter of peasants left and right throughout Central America. The main explanation for these social evolutions, one of the most important ones, is the lack of land.   There happens to be a land shortage in several of these countries under the given land tenure system. For you to simply state that the contrary is an empirical fact tells me that the rest of your paper is of the same calibre. There are a whole lot of assertions, empirical statements, that are simply incorrect.

Even more interesting, when you try to explain the causes of poverty, you carry on in the vein that you did a moment ago, stating that personal and cultural differences can account for economic poverty. Well, that is rather interesting. This is just the ideology that one would expect to hear from you. But that is hardly an explanation for international development of international capitalism or non-capitalism. I would suggest that if the main obstacles to economic development are personal, ideological and cultural, then what we ought to do is stop our aid programmes, send in 10,000 psychiatrists, and teach these people to have a better attitude. (laughter)

I think the title of your paper should be "Little Rabbit FooFoo, I Don't Like Your Attitude." To try in one paper, as you have, to explain the inter-relationships of development of capitalist/non-capitalist Third World countries, and to subsume it under a single factor, defies all logic. I find that incredible, absolutely astounding.

BERNARD ZAGORIN: Thank you sir. Professor Bauer, you have the floor.

SPEAKER #15: I just have one more comment and then I'll sit down.

The other comment is that the rest of the paper, for those of you who haven't seen it, is a diatribe against the Catholic church, which is interesting. They can defend themselves, I'm sure. But I actually found it quite insulting.

LORD BAUER: All right. I shall answer this little diatribe in reverse order from the way it was presented.

First, let me make clear what I mean by saying that personal, cultural, and social factors are major determinants of economic achievement. If you will look at countries where there are ethical/cultural differences between people who have access to the same natural resources, you will find very wide income differences. There will be both personal and group differences, among people with access to the same natural resources. Malaysia is one example. The Chinese and the Indians and the Malays are three distinct ethnic groups. The Chinese and the Indians came in as penniless coolies. They were much discriminated against by the British administration, in favour of the Malays. Nevertheless, they both vastly out-distanced, very quickly, the Malays in economic performance. As well, the Chinese also out-distanced the Indians although they both came in, as I say, as penniless and illiterate coolies.

Second, concerning the explanation of international differences in income, I would like to draw your attention to the fact that throughout the Third World the poorest and most backward groups, and we are speaking of material poverty, are those with no external contact or practically no external contact -- groups like aborigines, pygmies, tribal societies in Africa.

As regards the land tenure systems, I claim to know them pretty well in Africa and in Southeast Asia. In much of Africa, where the poorest people live, such as the tribal societies or the desert people, land, including cultivatable land, is a free good.

For Latin America, I am less well qualified to speak, much less so. But I have been to Guatemala and I have seen the situation. Two-thirds of the populace are native Indians. I do not know how much land was taken from them and, if so, under what conditions. What I do know is that in the Amazon valley, where extremely poor and backward populations live, there were very large areas where land is a free good, exactly as in Central Africa and Southeast Asia.

BERNARD ZAGORIN, CHAIRMAN: Thank you.

MURDITH MacLEAN: I think that when we speak of development, we also have to raise the question of dependency. When money is being transferred, the question is, who becomes dependent on whom? When two groups have contact with each other, the question becomes, is it really an honest exchange back and forth or is it in some way a distorted one, where one side has undue power over the other? Obviously, in any kind of a closed community system, the whole question of poverty doesn't arise because in that intimate setting everyone is in the same boat.

The recognition of poverty only comes as a result of contacts, as one sees groups with more and groups with less. At this point the awareness would come in and develop. I always think we have to raise the question of dependency. Who has been made dependent on whom, as these contacts take place?

BERNARD ZAGORIN, CHAIRMAN: Thank you. Yes, sir.

SPEAKER #16: I've listened to your last two panelists with considerable interest, but there is one thing that bothers me. Most of the panelists take an approach that really amounts to the rationalization of injustice. They should, rather, address themselves to the question of how justice can be found. Let me be more specific. I think if we look at North American society, which we would all agree is fairly wealthy, compared with Central and South American society, or the so-called Third World, we can see certain factors that make a very big contribution to injustice in both areas. And the questions that some of the young women were trying to address this morning can't be gotten around by questioning income distribution. There is injustice directed towards women in this society and to many other minority peoples in North American society. If we look at the developing world, we find the same factors which contribute to injustice in North America. While I know the Chairman is ready to cut me off, I'll just ask a brief question, which is this: I think that the $750 billion going to the arms race is feeding injustice in the whole globe and I would like to know if they are in favour of the expansion of the arms race or against it? Thank you.

RICK HORDERN: Against. But to address your first point, can poverty or injustice be measured by differentiation of incomes, I say that it can. I believe that when you talk about society, you are talking about an organic unit. Once there is any sort of imbalance in one place, it is going to cause disturbances elsewhere. Yes, absolute dollars and cents don't tell you how people are living and whether there is or is not poverty, or whether or not there is injustice. But in general, income discrepancy is a symptom of injustice. I also feel that justice is something that goes beyond purely economic questions; it deals with a variety of kinds of relations in society. These relations can get unbalanced for many kinds of reasons, in many kinds of ways. Yes, we'd like to see the arms race ended.

BERNARD ZAGORIN, CHAIRMAN: Thank you. Yes sir.

SPEAKER #17: I am an Associate Professor of Political Science here at the University. Mr. Chairman I wish to make a small remark about Professor Peter Bauer's comments in two regards. First, consider his analysis of the spiritual basis of Hinduism in which cattle cannot be killed. I am in fact amazed by the over-simplified understanding this portrays about the relationship of Indian society or Hindu society and not eating or killing cattle. His analysis is far too simplistic.

Second, I do take a strong exception to the use of such words as "niggers," which he has not used, but "coolies" in the case of the Malaysian society, which really means the two racial slurs which come from time to time from people who suffer from racist attitudes. And this is, of course, not in disagreement with this analysis of foreign aid. As a matter of fact, I agree to a large degree, in terms of the analysis he has why foreign aid must be rejected or should be rejected by the so-called recipient countries. Unfortunately, his pre-conceived notions, which may well be his theoretical notions in terms of why aid should be received, in my opinion, suffer from two limitations. One, I get a sense of racism in terms of his explanation of certain small productive ethnic composition of West African societies or other parts. Secondly, he is directing his analysis mainly against any socialized, any collective, any solidarity-oriented efforts of developing countries in combating the massive problems which they face. Otherwise, as I have said earlier, that aid must be rejected from rich countries to the poor countries; if it has to be received, it should be received as a right. In that sense I do reject the position taken by Professor MacLean because he has come to the...some kind of understanding that within Christianity the notion is that aid should be given ostensibly as charity but, of course, if it is charity then it contradicts Liberation Theology because where it exceeds the rule Christianity to fight oppression, fight injustice, and of course, go with the forces for social progress. So, unfortunately, what has happened that if Professor Hordern's position was not taken, both aid and charity are in the same direction and if it were not rejected on the grounds of what Professor Bauer has said earlier, because of practice he has described, aid should be supported. Aid should be supported to the resculization (sic) of Western domination of Third World countries as part of charity. For instance, Professor MacLean has just said, well, if the nations could be persuaded, the truth is that economic poverty, injustice and under-development in most of the Third World is a direct result of an unjust distribution of wealth and also the exploitation of the resources which actually belong to the Third World in general. So my question to Professor Bauer is, that the reasons for rejection of aid are acceptable as he has given but unfortunately he had is it because of the racial, cultural and other factors, he said that aid should be rejected?

And second question, to Professor MacLean is, "Why charity?" If it has to be accepted, couldn't it be in terms of the rights, in terms of either in the new international economic order or in terms of the just rights which have been denied to the Third World for..over a period time and it is time that that redressal (sic) should be done now.

BERNARD ZAGORIN, CHAIRMAN: Thank you. Professor Bauer.

LORD BAUER: Well, I can only reply to some of the points raised by the last speaker. I will try to reply to those which I think raise issues of the widest interest.

First, the question of racism. I don't quite know what it is that has become an issue. From where did this expression of abuse arise? To say that the Chinese in Malaysia came in as penniless labourers, that 95 per cent of them were illiterate, and that they have out-distanced the other groups in economic performance, has absolutely no trace of racism in it. It is merely an observation. And exactly the same can be said about Africa. For example, in Nigeria, the Ibo, who until the end of the 19th century, in fact, had never seen a modern civilization, have completely out-distanced the other groups. I don't quite know the explanation for this but I observe that this is so.

The last speaker brought forth another argument in favour of government-to-government wealth transfers; namely, restitution for historical wrongs, as recompense for Western misdeeds. We could talk about this until the cows come home, but let me point out that some of the poorest and most materially backward countries in the Third World have had no external contacts whatever. For example, in central Asia, this applies to countries like Sukkim, Bhutan, and Tibet. In Africa, there are the central African tribal societies, and there are two countries in West Africa which were never colonies, Liberia and Ethiopia -- and they are among the most backward. This is not at all a defence of colonialism, to which I object; it is simply a statement of fact.

I would also like to make a general point. I think it is a mistake to think that income differences generally reflect differences in political power. This is not so. Sometimes they do, but in the modern world this is exceptional. Look at the positions of Jews and non-conformists in Western Europe. The Jews had no political rights until the middle of the 19th century. By that time, however, they had become one of the richest groups in Europe. And substantially this applies to the position of the non-conformists in England. It applies also to material achievements of the Chinese in Southeast Asia, who not only have no political rights but were openly and systematically discriminated against by the British administration and subsequently by the Malays.

BERNARD ZAGORIN, CHAIRMAN: Thank you. Now, Professor MacLean.

MURDITH MacLEAN: I think I have been misunderstood. If that's my fault, let me try to clear this up -- although perhaps we may differ. I don't believe in charity. If I have what is yours or what is ours in common, and I return it to you, I do not give charity. I give you what is yours. And that is partly why I am saying that the Christian, and not just the Christian, view of things entails a duty to share -- not charity.

Second, we have to understand what really assists people and what does not. We have to listen carefully to the people to whom we are returning this wealth. We have to make sure that it really is of assistance. Here I would want to listen to what Professor Bauer and other economists have to tell us. Most important, we must listen to the people to whom this is meant to give assistance. I would be surprised though, if even in government-to-government transfers of wealth there aren't considerable alternatives, regarding the way in which the wealth is transferred, with what kinds of understandings and requirements. There are many kinds of government-funded schemes. For example, government might pay salaries to enable industrial assistance to be given to people to go from this country to other nations, at their request, and in the places for which they ask. I would have thought that those sorts of things are within the ambit of foreign aid. They are not charity and I think they stand a chance of working.

LORD BAUER: May I ask a question also of Professor MacLean? This is really not altogether a rhetorical question. How far does a Christian's duty to share depend on the circumstances of the giver and recipient, and in particular on the conduct of the recipient? It seems to me to say simply that income differences are sufficient to require sharing, leads to real anomalies, both on the micro level and on the macro or global level. Surely a man who is poor because he habitually overspends a large income is a different person from the one who has been stricken by illness or circumstances over which he has no control. And globally that applies, even much more so. Should East African governments be given aid by us when they have expelled their most productive subjects, causing immense hardship and thereby reducing per capita incomes? I mean that sharing in those circumstances simply enables them to continue in this fashion. And this indeed is exactly what is happening.

MURDITH MacLEAN: I agree. What I am trying to suggest is that income differences or differences in wealth are a prima facie case for sharing. Now it may be that the case is defeated by other circumstances. For instance, the person may decline it. Or the person may have chosen a way of proceeding that, in effect, cuts him off from benefiting from aid. There are lots of ways in which the prima facie case for sharing may be defeated by the particular factors and circumstances. All of this is quite true but I wanted to establish in the beginning that sharing is the first thing to be considered; and it arises not because of charity from the individual who possesses wealth to one who doesn't, but because of the human condition which requires sharing.

BERNARD ZAGORIN, CHAIRMAN: Professor Hordern.

RICK HORDERN: I think that the basic Christian concept of giving is that it is without strings attached. Apart from the question of the morality of the recipient, I think that has always been the pattern in which God acts in the first place towards people. And it seems to me that the basic pattern we look at in terms of the work of the churches is--is there a need? If there is a need, we try to meet that need and work at it. One doesn't raise the question of how moral is the government. Rather, one tries to meet that need. One doesn't raise the question of whether things could have been different. Maybe they could have, and maybe not.

SPEAKER #18: I'm a housewife and a university student. I would like to address two issues, one of which is materialism or economic wealth, and the other is guilt.

As I understand it, poverty relates to a situation where people do not have enough food to eat and clothing to wear. One of the burdens we have as Western people is materialism. We don't understand people who are not interested in as much materialism as we. So one of the things we turn to is religion and we are really searching for something. I suppose we could call it peace of mind. But what religion tends to give us is guilt. This is because of our materialistic wealth. So, we are caught in a bind, and I am not sure from whom the aid should flow. I'm not sure if it's from us to the Third World people or if we, in fact, need to learn something from the Third World people. One example of this reverse exchange was in the news recently. A group in Glasgow, Scotland has requested that Mother Theresa come and teach them some of the things that she has been teaching to those in Calcutta. They felt that perhaps they could learn something from what she had to offer.

BERNARD ZAGORIN, CHAIRMAN: Thank you. I take it that was addressed to every member of the panel.

SPEAKER #18: Yes, it is. But I think it related most of all to what Lord Bauer had to say in the beginning.

LORD BAUER: I think these are very interesting questions, which raise very wide moral issues. The specific point I would like to make is this. A feeling of guilt is a very unsatisfactory basis for a policy of official aid or indeed, in actual fact, for any other aid. This is because people who feel guilty and give aid or suggest that aid should be given are more concerned with their own emotional state, with their own mental state, rather than with the effect of the policy which they support.

If I may introduce a personal note, I was recently in the Sudan. I visited the Southern Sudan with its hundreds of thousands of refugees from other African countries, especially from poor African countries. A number of the poor countries are Ethiopia, Uganda, Zaire and Chad. Voluntary agencies are doing wonderful work among these refugees. But their resources are trivial compared to the enormous volume of Western aid to all these four governments. And this official Western aid to the African governments is inspired, to a considerable degree, by guilt feelings. This is a very unsure guide to policy because it is concerned, as I say, with your own mental state and with that of your fellow citizens, and not with the effect or the repurcussion of the policy.

Now, as regards Mother Theresa whose institution I actually visited in Calcutta. She is doing absolute wonders but I think she would be out of her depth in Scotland, if that's what you said.

BERNARD ZAGORIN, CHAIRMAN: Professor Hordern.

RICK HORDERN: Yes, religion and guilt are often associated. But I think there is a difference between healthy and un-healthy guilt. I encourage everyone to feel guilty in a healthy way. But obviously guilt can become unhealthy, in which case it is not good. In terms of actions, the motive really never should be simply guilt or fear. Rather, it should be based on love. Yet I don't think we can simply ignore these questions. Guilt also reminds us of the realities, that we live in a world with other people. Guilt means we are aware that we have broken some sort of standard or relation with these other people. In the healthy sense, this can prod us to be aware of our short-comings. Hopefully, though, love would always be the motive for the giving.

MURDITH MacLEAN: I just want to add something to what Professor Bauer said. Although I think it is true that guilt is a dangerous emotion to act on by itself, it does not logically follow that one shouldn't act on it at all. I think the consequence should be that we act on guilt with great care.

The fact is, there are times when guilt is justified, and we have to be sure that it is justified. But when it is, then I think the reminder is well-administered. Then, people should act on it with care and wisdom, being "wise as serpents." Just because we are acting from guilt, and any action I undertake might be unwise, it by no means follows that we should not act at all. I am sure that this is not what Professor Bauer would suggest.

BERNARD ZAGORIN, CHAIRMAN: Thank you. Yes, sir.

SPEAKER #19: I work with the University of Regina Extension. I have a comment and a question for Lord Peter Bauer. I found myself in agreement with quite a lot of what you said, sir, about the limitations or the ineffectiveness of bilateral aid, government-to-government aid. But I was hoping that you would go further in terms of those limitations. It is hard to deny, I think, that the aid given after World War II by the United States to Japan and Germany, for example, produced some pretty remarkable effects. But if we look at the situation right now, for example, the economic and military aid going from the United States to other countries, it's very different. I would like you to comment on just how this, in fact, does prevent or distort true development. I am thinking, for example, of American aid to El Salvador, to the Philippines, and other South American countries like Brazil. It seems to me that bilateral aid has had a very serious effect on the development of those countries in terms of distorting their development in a human fashion.

One last point: consider the question of guilt as a motivation with respect to Zaire, for example. It does raise the question of whether a rich country like Zaire is motivated out of guilt or whether there might possibly be some other less altruistic reasons involved. This goes for the Philippines as well. I think we often find particular benefits in the donor country, whether it is a strategic military base or certain kinds of mineral wealth. This pertains to a previous commentator who referred to a flow in reverse. I think you could expand that also to the flow, not only of ideas from the Third World back to the donor countries, but also to the fact that the net economic flow in some cases is in this direction rather than the other direction. Would you be able to comment on some of those points?

LORD BAUER: Certainly, and I would like to start by commenting on your first point, perhaps at some length because it is always at the back of the minds of North Americans. Let us analyze the success of the Marshall aid to Europe and the corresponding aid to Japan. How does this compare with aid to the Third World? There is an absolutely fundamental difference, which is this: The economies of Western Europe had to be restored, not developed. The performance of these economies before the war -- or these societies, I should say -- made it clear that the people had the faculties, the culture, and the political institutions suitable for material progress. Now, this makes it clear why it was possible to terminate Marshall aid to Germany in four years and for Germany to became an exporter of capital two years later. This occurred in spite of the fact that, over these four years, West Germany had to absorb ten million refugees from the East, among whom old people and young children were disproportionately represented. And Germany had lost at least three million men, of its most productive age group, as prisoners of war in the Soviet Union. As well, during this period Germany had to pay reparations to the Soviet Union. With all this it was possible to terminate Marshall aid, which actually wasn't so great. Compare that with the present aid programmes which are envisaged to extend into the 21st century. One British Minister of Overseas Development told me that he thought it would extend even beyond the 21st century. We are here in a completely different area. That's the most important of the points you raised with me.

Secondly, you said Zaire is a rich country. This is quite interesting. Zaire has one of the lowest per capita incomes in the world. Therefore, what you may mean is that there may be valuable minerals in that country. That is very different. The fact that you referred to it as a rich country, when it has one of the lowest per capita incomes, underlines the point I made earlier -- that natural resources on their own are of very little value.

BERNARD ZAGORIN, CHAIRMAN: Thank you.

SPEAKER # 20: I farm near Regina. My question is directed to Professor Hordern. You mentioned in your presentation that you disagreed somewhat with Marxist concepts of materialism and atheism. But you said nothing about the extent to which the church might disagree with their reliance upon the use of violence as a means of attaining political ends.

I should perhaps quote very briefly from the final paragraph of their manifesto. "Communists disdain to conceal their views and aims. They openly declare that their aims can be attained only by the forcible overthrow of all existing social conditions." Now this has manifested itself clearly. Wherever you find Marxism you also find violence, on an almost perpetual basis. You have the thousands and thousands of communists killing each other in the Soviet Union in the 1930s and so on. The Russians end up fighting the Chinese, the Chinese fighting the Cambodians or the Vietnamese, and the Vietnamese fighting the Cambodians. You have Marxism in Grenada. Bishop wasn't murdered by the right. He was murdered by one of his own leftists. How does the modern church defend its association and its promotion, even adoption, of this use of violence as a means of attaining political goals? I would like to hear your comments on that.

RICK HORDERN: Well, first of all I would say that violence, in and of itself, is not intrinsic to Marxism. Marxists see violence as appropriate when certain conditions are present, but they feel it futile to try to force a revolution when the time isn't ready. It is simply seen as an extension of political power in particular situations. One can therefore be a Marxist, or adopt many Marxist ideals, apart from the question of violence. Also, I think we should note there is never political change without struggle. Take the case of Chile. There, the attempt to establish a Marxist government democratically was actually thwarted by other powers in the world. It was really the United States which perpetuated the violence there. The attitude of the churches today is not to favour violence but rather to discourage it. The church always seeks a peaceful resolution to a conflict. But we must recognize that people in the churches often feel the time has come when the injustices are so great, when there is already violence being done in terms of say malnutrition and oppression against the poor, that people will be justified in engaging in political violence. It is a reluctant position, but it is one, especially in Latin America, that's often seen.

BERNARD ZAGORIN, CHAIRMAN: Ladies and gentlemen, it is now ten after five. Let me thank all the panelists and the audience for their participation. But we must now end this session.

ETHICAL REFLECTIONS ON THE ECONOMIC CRISIS

DR. WALTER BLOCK

JOSEPH GAVIN, CHAIRMAN: Let us begin. We will adopt the same format as was used this afternoon, and we will begin in the order stated on the programme, alphabetically. We will call upon Dr. Walter Block to begin. Dr. Block is the Director of the Centre for the Study of Economics and Religion of the Fraser Institute. Dr. Block.

WALTER BLOCK: I would like to address myself to the topic of the evening, "Ethical Reflections on the Economic Crisis." However, there were one or two things that came up on previous panels. Such as Gunnar Myrdal on rent control, and women's wages, and income distribution, so I hope that I will have some time to get involved with these questions, perhaps during the discussion period.

I have written a full reply to the paper written by the Canadian Conference of Catholic Bishops, Ethical Reflections on the Economic Crisis. It is called Focus: On Economics and the Canadian Bishops. Unfortunately I can't give you the whole story here. Instead I will confine myself to one very important highlight and subsequently touch on a few other points very briefly. Let me first say that I find this a welcome statement of the Catholic bishops. Even though I don't agree with much of it, I welcome the document. I think it is very important that this monograph has been printed and published and widely circulated to the Canadian public. It is highly moral in its focus and in its intentions. It focuses a moral spotlight on a hitherto bloodless economic statistic, one that meant little or nothing to most people. I refer to the unemployment rate. We can no longer, I contend, thanks to the bishops, sweep these unemployment figures under the rug. It has now become meaningful to us in a way that was impossible but for the efforts of the bishops, and for that, and much more, I applaud them.

Moreover, Ethical Reflections on the Economic Crisis has been highly criticized and I think very unfairly. My own criticism, of course, is all fair. (laughter) The bishops have been criticized because they are not economists. You know, the bishops, aren't economists and therefore they should keep quiet. Well, I think that the day when economists attain a monopoly power over speaking on economics will be a very sad day for Canada. I think that everyone should have free speech rights, even bishops. (laughter)

I especially welcome their preferential option for the poor. That is their first principle. I accept this wholeheartedly -- as a goal. Of what, then, do my criticisms consist? My criticisms are, broadly speaking, that the means adopted and urged by the bishops to achieve this goal, namely, the preferential option for the poor, are unfortunately misdirected. That is, those policies that they say will help the poor, will actually harm them. The means that they have adopted not only will not lead to the goal of alleviating poverty, they will lead in many cases to the diametric opposite of that to which they are aiming. The goal is fine, the means are problematic.

Labour Unions

Let me concentrate on one of the five short-term strategies proposed by the bishops. "Labour unions should be asked to play a more decisive and responsible role in developing strategies for economic recovery and unemployment." Let us concentrate on only one aspect of labour unionism, its advocacy of minimum wage laws. This is especially important in this particular context since the Fraser Institute has recently been criticized by some people in Regina for opposing the minimum wage law. In the view of these people if you are against this legislation, you are anti-people. Well, I hope to demonstrate to you that this is not so. On the contrary, if you are pro-people and take seriously the bishops' preferential option for the poor, then you have to oppose the minimum wage law. How do we begin?

Let us suppose that the minimum wage law is pegged at $4 per hour. Actually, this level varies. In some provinces it's $3.50, $3.60, in others as much as $4.50. But let's just assume that the minimum wage law is $4 per hour. We must see this situation from the vantage point of a person whose productivity is only $1 per hour. That is to say, such a person can produce, by dint of his best efforts, goods worth only $1 per hour. And what is the vantage point of the employer who is thinking of hiring him? On the one hand, the employer must pay this man $4 per hour because that is the amount required by law. On the other hand, the amount that he can derive from employing this person is only $1 per hour. Simple arithmetic will convince us readily that if the employer hires this person at $4 per hour, he will lose $3 per hour.

Now, the employer might be a Christian businessman or a religious businessman or a Good Samaritan and hire him anyway, and take the loss. If so, he would lose $3 an hour for every hour that this man works for him. And he might even hire two or three such people. Can he hire 500 such people? Well, unless he is very, very wealthy indeed, he will go broke if he tries. In any case, that is not the way he achieved his wealth in the first place -- not by making losses on his decisions.

More is Better?

Suppose, now, that the minimum wage law were not $4 an hour but rather (on the principle that if a little bit of the minimum wage law is good, a lot is better), that the Province of Saskatchewan raised the minimum wage law to $100 per hour. Now which of us in this auditorium, ladies and gentlemen, or anywhere in the province, for that matter, can produce at the rate of $100 per hour? The productivity of most people is far less than that. It could be $20 or $30 an hour. Consider the plight of the person who can produce $25 per hour. If he is hired at $100 an hour his employer will lose $75, and he will not be hired. I put it to you that if we had a minimum wage law at $100 per hour, virtually everyone in the province would be unemployed. Well, it doesn't work that way with a minimum wage law of only $4 an hour. But still $4 an hour is quite a high barrier to employment for people down in the bottom rungs of skill levels.

The minimum wage law is an <u>unemployment</u> law. It is not an <u>employment</u> law. The minimum wage law says, if we can borrow the biblical way of speaking, "thou shalt not employ anyone for less than $4 an hour." It doesn't talk about who thou shalt employ, it just says "thou shalt not employ anyone who is paid less than $4 an hour." If you can picture employment as a step ladder, this is like cutting off the bottom rungs of the ladder. We are telling people who are standing on the ground that if you want to get onto the employment ladder, you have got to catapult, you have got to pole vault, up to the third or fourth rung of the employment ladder. You cannot take teeny bits and steps up the employment ladder, one at a time.

Gradualism

In a previous manifestation in my life, I was once a swimming and diving instructor. I would teach people to dive by telling them to walk down the step ladder into the pool, stand on the bottom rung, and then dive off. At this point, the water was up to their necks. It was absolutely no threat to them, so they could do that easily. Then I suggested that they move up just one step. Now the water reached to their chests. Again, diving off was no big deal. The process continued step by step. Eventually, they could launch themselves off from higher and higher diving boards. Well, I want to make an analogy between my diving lessons and employment. If you insist that a person must jump to a high level of employment, and skip the first few rungs, you put great pressure on him. It is very difficult. If you let him take teeny steps, a low-paid job where he might receive the training necessary to prepare him for a higher level job, he will not have as great difficulty.

There is a Catch 22 situation. Most employers demand experience before they will hire a young person. But the young person can't get the experience without the job in the first place. Now, in the old days, the Horatio Alger days, things were different. If the employer didn't want to hire our

Horatio Alger, a young, heroic type person, if he was fearful that Alger didn't have the necessary experience, our boy would look the man straight in the eye and say, "Look, you don't have to take the risk. Hire me for half pay, or a penny a day, or I will even work for you for free for a day or for a week, and then you'll see how good I am. Give me this chance and I'll work without you bearing the risk." And in that way Alger could get the job.

But do you know what would happen to a modern-day Horatio Alger who tried that? He would go to jail along with any employer who took him up on his offer. Because they would be violating the minimum wage law. Look, it's a choice. The choice for this person (whose productivity is $1 per hour) is employment at the low level of $1 per hour or unemployment at the relatively princely rate of $4 per hour. Now which is better? To earn $1 per hour from employment, or to earn zero from unemployment at the minimum wage law of $4 per hour?

Who Is Hurt?

Who does this affect? It affects the unskilled, the uneducated, teenagers, people with special problems, native peoples, for example. The proof of this can be seen in our general unemployment rate. The general unemployment rate for all Canadians is only 8, 9, 10, 11, 12 per cent. It fluctuates in that range. But do you know what the unemployment rate is for unskilled people -- people intimately affected by the minimum wage law? It is the highest recorded unemployment rate for all Canada. It is in the double digits. It's in the 25/30 per cent range. And even this is an underestimate of the real problem. For the way our unemployment statistics are constructed, you are only counted as unemployed if you are actively seeking a job. But suppose you have been actively seeking a job and you are unable to find it. Well, you are not counted as unemployed, then.

I have one minute left, so let me give you one further example, babysitting. Imagine if they passed a law requiring that babysitters be paid $4 an hour. This would play havoc. Young girls would find great difficulties. Why is it so hard to see this? Why is it so hard to understand the economics of the minimum wage law? Well one reason for this, I would contend, is that many people say, well, you can starve really starve on $1 per hour. The answer to that, of course, is that you don't really have to change the welfare system. For example, suppose that welfare is $100 per week and that this is invariant whether we have a minimum wage law or not. Now which is better? Receiving $100 per week in welfare and zero from employment for a grand total of $100? Or, receiving the same $100 a week in welfare plus $1 per hour times 40 hours for a total of $40 from employment for a total of $140? Obviously, the latter is preferable.

I've just run out of time. Thank you.

JOSEPH GAVIN, CHAIRMAN: Thank you Dr. Block.

ETHICAL REFLECTIONS ON THE ECONOMIC CRISIS

DR. REX BODA

JOSEPH GAVIN, CHAIRMAN: I now call Dr. Rex Boda to the microphone. Dr. Boda is the President of the Canadian Bible College in Regina.

REX BODA: This evening I would like to comment on the subject before us, "Ethical Reflections on the Economic Crisis." I shall do so from three perspectives: the biblical, the historical, and the contemporary.

It has been the constant view of the Judeo-Christian heritage that a follower of the God of Abraham, Isaac and Jacob, one who has entered into a living relationship with that God, will be a person whose faith leads to social concern and social action. This viewpoint is seen in every part of the Old and New Testaments. You can see this if you take the time to go through those pages. When the people of God cease to remember and to practice this essential application of their faith, then, the threat of the Lord is that they will be called "not my people."

I say that the Scriptures consistently speak in this fashion through the voice of their many prophets. We recognize that Jesus was quoting Moses when He spoke of the two great commandments which you have all heard. Moses said in the book of Deuteronomy 6:5, "Love the Lord thy God, your God, with all your heart and with all your soul and with all your strength." That is the first commandment and the second is like unto it, "Love your neighbour as yourself." Moses in the Pentateuch dealt with the issues of social justice. I note especially that passage in Leviticus 19 which contained the love thy neighbour comment. We are instructed in that chapter, in these words, verse 11, "do not steal." Or verse 13, "do not defraud your neighbour, or rob him, do not hold back the wages of a hired man overnight." Or verse 15, "do not pervert justice, do not show partiality to the poor or favouritism to the great, but judge your neighbour fairly." Verse 16, "do not do anything that endangers your neighbour's life." And the prophet seals it with this, "I am the Lord speaking on behalf of God." And then finally in verse 18, "Love your neighbour as yourself."

Practice Justice

Jesus, of course, quoted these passages when he was asked which were the greatest commandments. And often in the early church, and in the Epistles of the New Testament, the second commandment was seen as the practical application of the first. Reference to it was enough to summarize the whole responsibility, at times. This is true especially in the writings of Paul. Going back to the Old Testament, in the Psalms, I note the passage in Psalm 146, five through nine, which gives us a picture of the nature and the character of the God of Israel. In these words, "Thus it is he whose help is the God of Jacob, whose hope is in the Lord his God, the maker of heaven and earth the sea and everything in them. The Lord who remains faithful forever. He upholds the cause of the oppressed and gives food to the hungry. The Lord sets prisoners free. The Lord gives sight to the blind. The Lord lifts up those who are bowed down. The Lord loves the righteous. The Lord watches over the alien and sustains the fatherless and widows but he is frustrated for he frustrates the way of the wicked." This holds as well if we go on to the Prophets of the Old Testament, both the major and minor Prophets. They are full of exortations to practice justice. Let Mica summarize their messages in Mica 6:8: "He has showed you all man what is good and what does the Lord require of you? To act justly and to love mercy. And to walk humbly with your God."

Turning to the New Testament, we have already noted some of the words of Jesus and we could expand on that as far as giving the cup of cold water in His name. We come to the thinking of Paul and his writings. I note that in the words of Titus, speaking of Jesus Christ, he said this, "Who gave himself for us to redeem us from all wickedness and to purify for himself a people that are his very own. Either to do what is good." And finally in that very practical epistle of James, the rather renowned practical book on Christian living, we read, at the end of the first chapter, that "religion that God our father accepts is pure and faultless is thus." There is this, "to look after orphans and widows in their distress and keep oneself from being polluted by the world." And the next chapter of James says, "you show me your faith without your works and I'll show you my faith by my works."

Ministering to the Needy

I think these citations accurately reflect the consistent message of the Scriptures to those who would follow the God of the Scriptures -- that we are to do justice, to practice justice. We are to defend the fatherless and the widows and the oppressed. And the high points of church history have come as the church addressed its thinking and ministered to the needs and problems confronting the man or woman in the street or on the farm, be they spiritual, emotional, physical or material. The early church instructed its people to function in a harsh and an oppressive society, and how to minister to that society. The result was that society became more humane. In the long view this allowed them to function in their integrity as individuals created in the image of God.

In my own tradition, the leaders of the Reformation were confronted with economic controls of their people. They answered in varying ways at times, as can be seen by looking at the total Reformation and later developments in the various evangelical movements. These revivals led to confrontation with a variety of societal concerns and the result was specfic actions. For example the ministries of John Wesley, the Methodist, and of George Woodfield, the Evangelist, their associates and their successors, led to the establishment of orphanages. These met the needs of the under-privileged created in England with an exploited labour force (which lead to the struggle against slavery in the various British parliaments.) This applied to a John Howard working for prison reform, to a Shaftsbury working for improvement of conditions in factories. My own denomination started when our founder began a ministry to immigrants in New York City. This was not enthusiastically endorsed by the church of which he was then the pastor.

Social Guidelines

On the current scene, there can be no doubt that we are facing a crisis in the economic realm which must be faced, and which must be addressed in an effective fashion. Members of the evangelical community which I represent have been discussing these issues and have attempted to create some guidelines in our social responsibility. At a consultation called by the World Evangelical Fellowship in June of 1982, this statement was issued: "We are appalled to know that about 800 million people, or one-fifth of the human race, are destitute, lacking the basic necessities for survival, and that thousands of them die of starvation every day. Many more millions are without adequate shelter and clothing, without clean water and health care, without opportunities for education and employment, and are condemned to eke out a miserable existence without the possibility of self-improvement for themselves or their families. They can only be described as 'oppressed' by the gross economic inequality from which they suffer and the diverse economic systems which cause and perpetuate it.

"The oppression of others is political. They are denied fundamental human rights by totalitarian regimes of the extreme left or right, while if they protest they are imprisoned without trial, tortured, and killed. Yet others suffer discrimination on account of their race or sex. And all of us are oppressed by global problems which seem to defy solution -- conditions of overpopulaton and famine, the exploitation of non-renewable resources of energy, the spoilation of the environment, community violence, war and the ever-present threat of a nuclear holocaust.

"All these are rooted in the profound sinfulness of humankind, and they demand from the people of God a radical response of compassion. Only the Gospel can change human hearts, and no influence makes people more human than the

Gospel does. Yet we cannot stop with verbal proclamation. In addition to worldwide evangelization, the people of God should become deeply involved in relief, aid, development and the quest for social justice and peace."

And to do these things is the practice the inescapable ethic of our Lord. To do any less is unethical, is immoral, and I think, it probably could be said, is obscene.

JOSEPH GAVIN, CHAIRMAN: Thank you Dr. Boda.

ETHICAL REFLECTIONS ON THE ECONOMIC CRISIS

FATHER ISIDORE GORSKI

JOSEPH GAVIN, CHAIRMAN: I now call the Rev. Professor Isidore Gorski to the microphone. Father Gorski is Professor of Humanities and Religious Studies at Campion College.

ISIDORE GORSKI: As Dr. Block mentioned in his opening remarks, more than any other single issue, unemployment dominates the statement of the Canadian Conference of Catholic Bishops issued in January 1983. Both in the broader church's social thinking, and in the specific position of the Canadian bishops, employment is seen as a central issue in the economy because it is so important for human dignity. A belief in the special dignity that is inherent in every human person is the starting point for most of the church's reflections on economic issues.

Now this is particularly true in the case of unemployment. Our national economic life in Canada is currently the most critical setting in the struggle to achieve greater human dignity. The formation of economic policy, therefore, is far too important, to be left solely to technicians, to market forces, or to interest groups like the Fraser Institute. As someone once said, "war is too important to be left to the generals." To paraphrase, "the economic order is too important to be left to the economists." The workings of the economy have implications far beyond the maketplace, the boardroom, and the stock exchange.

Behind the jumble of statistics and the rise and fall of economic indicators lie human lives and individual tragedies. I think it was Stalin who made the statement, "a thousand deaths is a statistic, one death is a tragedy." You can say the same about the whole question of unemployment. We are always quoting statistics and percentages, but I submit that behind each unemployed person there is a real human and tragic problem. It is precisely for these reasons that economic issues are also moral issues. The basic test of economic policy is how it affects human persons -- how it promotes or denies human dignity and the common good. Employment issues are at the heart of economic analysis from the church's point of view because work is seen to have a special dignity. It is linked to the very meaning of life. Work is, in the words of Pope John Paul, in his most recent encyclical, "a key, probably the essential key to the whole social question." Through work human beings express themselves, actualize themselves. They become more human, more capable of taking responsibility for their lives. Through working, men and women actually participate in creation. They share in God's work. Human labour, therefore, is enobling because it contributes to the dignity of the human person and to the fulfillment of God's plan for creation.

Evil Unemployment

From this perspective, therefore, unemployment is a particularly serious evil. And Dr. Block has as good as acknowledged that. It ranks very high on the church's list of economic issues to be addressed. Church leaders, and Catholic bishops in particular, neither claim to be, nor want to be, technical experts on employment. Their contribution to the economic policy debate is not to propose new technical solutions to complex problems such as unemployment and inflation. Rather, their role is to participate in the debate by calling attention to the moral values and the choices inherent in economic policy-making.

Given the church's concern about unemployment as an issue with important moral dimensions, what have been some of the more specific contributions of church leaders to the public policy debate on this issue?

First, church statements on unemployment have helped to call attention to the human aspect, and to the social costs of unemployment. For those who speak from a religious tradition, based on the dignity of the human person, this may appear to be an obvious theme. In the larger public debate, however, it is not so obvious. The technicians, the economists, and the politicians frequently become so absorbed in statistics, budget projections and numerical cost/benefit analyses that the human dimension and the social costs become obscured. Human dignity, after all, is not easily quantifiable. The personal and social costs of unemployment are not readily captured by the dollar sign. As a result, they don't easily fit into the economic equation and the budget ledgers that tend to dominate economic policy debate. It is for this reason that church statements have repeatedly called attention to the social and the human costs of unemployment. And we always will.

Inequitable Distribution

A second contribution which the church has attempted to make to the debate about unemployment is to emphasize that joblessness is inequitably distributed. Joblessness does not strike at random. Unemployment strikes disproportionately at those who are weakest in economic terms and at those who are subject to discrimination.

There is a third contribution that the Catholic church brings to the debate over unemployment. This is a focus on the larger picture. While commenting repeatedly on specific economic problems and crises, church statements have also raised deeper structural questions about the economy and the fundamental transformations affecting Canadian economic life. From the time of Rerum Novarum, which was the first social encyclical of the Catholic church, and issued by Leo XIII in 1891, to the most recent encyclical on human work, issued by Pope John Paul II, the church's social teaching has grappled with the underlying assumptions of various economic systems. Topics such as the role of private property, the maldistribution of wealth and ownership, the role of government and the rights of workers have been common themes in the encyclical tradition. Criticizing both extreme collectivism on the left and pure capitalism on the right, the church has consistently urged the pursuit of new economic structures that put the economy at the service of the human person and enhance both the common good and individual human dignity and freedom. In this debate which the statement of the Canadian bishops has participated, the issues of contention do not lie in problems such as whether or not there should be rent control, or how much rent control there should be. The real issue is, does capital have priority or does labour have priority? The Canadian bishops insist on the priority of labour over capital, and I think they will always insist on that.

Thank you.

ETHICAL REFLECTIONS ON THE ECONOMIC CRISIS

FATHER JAMES SCHALL

JOSEPH GAVIN, CHAIRMAN: I now invite Dr. James Schall to the microphone. Father Schall, a Jesuit, is Professor of Government and Political Philosophy at Georgetown University in Washington.

JAMES SCHALL: Thank you Father Gavin.

First of all, let me say a word of appreciation for the conference itself. I appreciate particularly the sponsorship of the university, here, and the attendance. I am quite impressed that there are this many people here. The quality of the questioning has been excellent and the interest shown has been magnificent. To me at least, this is a very impressive and vital sign of intellectual interest and concern.

I would like to do a couple of things in this talk. I have prepared a written address, but I don't think I'll give you the one I wrote, for various reasons. What I thought I would do first is make a comment, my own comment, a question which is, I think, of great pertinence. It has to do with the propriety of criticizing Catholic popes and bishops for positions they take on economics or politics. It seems to me that one ought to ask oneself first, to what audience are we talking when we are talking about criticizing a pope or a bishop or even a lowly Jesuit. (laughter) What is the audience? If it is the university audience, if it is an academic audience, the presupposition is intellectual; the presumption is one of integrity and freedom. And the Catholic church, it seems to me, historically, and indeed in practically any document in which this issue is discussed, has always taken the following position: that it is important and vital for people who disagree, whether they be within the church or Protestants, Jews, Muslims, whatever they may be, and this includes total non-believers, to state fairly and correctly and as bluntly as they wish what their problems are with the position of the Catholic church, or with a given individual in the church.

To do this, in my view, is not in any sense to insult the dignity or the stature or the status of the person or the author to whom you are addressing yourself. Now it is obviously possible, even for a professor, to be unfair and snide and bitter. We know that happens. But in general, an honest man says, "I have read the position of the Catholic church and I have the following difficulties with it which to me are very serious." Within the tradition of the Catholic church, it seems to me, and within the tradition of the intellectual integrity of which they ought to be obliged, one should say, "I appreciate very much the honour you do to us, to me, to state what you hold and why you hold it." And in the context of academic freedom and intellectual integrity, one can respond to that.

Academic Freedom

This is the very nature of academic freedom; that is why a university is a different kind of a place, really. It is why government and business, the lower schools and other such institutions are really not the same as a university. A university ought to be the kind of place where these kinds of questions can be asked, where people are able to respond to them. And the response should be gentle, intelligent, appreciative, convincing. But at the same time one ought to respect the fact that very often we solve problems only many years after the question was asked. St. Thomas, as you know, in the very structure of the Suma Theologica, has always been a kind of model. For the most part, on any issue that he took up he was able to state and felt his obligation to state, the objection to a thesis even better than most people who themselves maintained it. That is to say, we do not really fully understand a truth unless we fully understand a clear and honourable objection to that truth.

Now, I say this in a specific context. It is a very important thing both within religion and academia to protect that sense of fairness, bluntness and...I almost want to say the "no-holds-barredness" that belongs to honest intellectual discourse. There is nothing wrong with that. And it seems to me that it is important for us to uphold that tradition.

I now turn to the next point. What is the status of economic and political questions within the Catholic tradition? Let me say a word about that. Within the Catholic tradition, the Roman Catholic tradition, economics, politics, physics, chemistry, are not properly speaking, objects of revelation. Now there are going to be other views, Protestant views, which are not going to agree with that. Catholics, by virtue of the principle I just mentioned, have a great duty to respect and understand the reasons for this. Within the Catholic tradition on politics and economics, things are <u>not</u> to be discovered directly from scripture or from theological reflection and tradition. This doesn't mean that theology is not important. It is. But not all things are revealed to us, at least in our view. It is thus the obligation of mankind to discover and to gradually come to know what is true and what is false by virtue of its own experience, its own reflection, its own knowledge, in these areas.

Obligation to the Truth

The questions: what is economics? or what is political philosophy? or political science? or what is chemistry? are relatively late arrivals on the scene, so to speak. When people attend a modern university, and begin to look at all of the faculties, some say there is a revelation of anthropology and psychology and other disciplines. The important thing to recognize is that this is a very important aspect of Christian, or at least of Catholic understanding of its obligations to the truth. We must recognize that the political, economic and sociological sciences are themselves autonomous in the sense that they legitimately must discover their own principles and their own direction.

This is not to denegrate revelation. Indeed, it is to enhance revelation. Revelation may indeed have something to say to that; at least, I would say that revelation in one sense <u>means</u> this. It means there are truths directly addressed to our intelligence when we reflect upon them. In other words, any revealed doctrine directed to our intelligence ought to stimulate us to think better. As St. Thomas says in one of his discussions on this question, this is one of the purposes of revelation, and one of its indirect effects. We can in fact think better than we do. We are obliged to deal with what we do not fully comprehend. If we do, we become the beneficiaries of a sort of revelation. But this will not happen unless we seriously try as best we can to comprehend for ourselves. Our own individual minds can benefit, as well as can the minds of our confreres.

Wide Divergency

Now to return to economics and politics. Economics and politics are disciplines and experiences and realities in which there is wide, wide divergency. There is a legitimate wide divergency of views as to what ought to be done to solve our problems. In one sense these views can be looked upon as the distinction between justice and injustice. But they can also be looked upon in an alternative way. Almost as a matter of style. And it may be important to look upon it in this way.

For example, a distinction might be between the way the Italians drive a car, and the way the Germans drive a car, and the way the Americans drive a car, and the way that Canadians ski. (laughter) I read an article today about the Canadian skiers who are supposed to be, what did they call them, reckless. (laughter) That is the Canadian reputation. Here, the style differences are a good thing. It is a good thing that this variety is a part of our human existence. That is to say, we can form ourselves in different ways, in different directions. It isn't necessary that we all do everything absolutely and identically the same way. Justice can be done in many, many ways and still be justice. This can be so without denying the distinction between justice and injustice.

That having being said, I think it important to recognize that there is much at stake. The social doctrine of the church is not intended to deny the legitimate problems that exist in human history. First of all we must know what politics and economics are all about. Secondly, we must not deny the wide scope of diverse and legitimate choices which exist for mankind.

Economic Development

In closing, I want to say a couple of words on the question of economic development -- on the problems that we have been talking about today. I think there is a valid minority position which argues that the reason that the poor are poor is not because the rich are rich. Indeed, 200 years ago everyone, relatively speaking, was poor. The real problem is not why are the poor poor. The question is, why is not everyone poor? The answer to that is the key problem with a good part of Catholic and Protestant social thought. This literature is guilty of inattention to the concept of productivity. It ignores what causes wealth, what causes jobs, what causes labour, and what causes economic growth. You cannot really have an adequate distribution of wealth without paying full attention to productivity and its causes.

I don't say, of course, that this is the most important thing in human existence. It is not. One of the key premises in the history of political philosophy, and particularly the history of the Judeo/Christian tradition, is that the state is not of ultimate importance. Therefore, the very limitation of the state is itself dependent upon something else to which all of us are called, which is higher than the state.

There are political theories which deny that. And there are several such political philosophies, Marxism for example. Here it is denied that there are any kind of authorities or realities higher than the state. These theories tend to subsume all of the questions open to mankind to the political order. Aristotle said that if man were the highest being, politics would be the highest science. He also said, however, that politics, or man, is not the highest being. Therefore, we need a theory which follows the logic of this kind of argument. That is, we must restore the idea that human beings need not be hostile to one another because of wealth-producing profiteers.

Thank you.

JOSEPH GAVIN, CHAIRMAN: Thank you Dr. Schall.

ETHICAL REFLECTIONS ON THE ECONOMIC CRISIS

DISCUSSION

JOSEPH GAVIN, CHAIRMAN: Ladies and gentlemen, we now invite you to address the panelists. As you know, there are two microphones. Since this gentleman has already reached this one, we shall begin over here. But first, may I remind you once again to be relatively brief? Please direct your questions to one of the panelists or all the panelists unless you wish to make general observations. You might introduce yourself, if you so wish.

SPEAKER #21: I represent, I hope, the people of common sense. I want first of all, and I think this appropriate, to congratulate the Fraser Institute for this wonderful conference we have had here today. (Applause) I don't believe in everything they advocate, far from it. Nor do I believe everything economists advocate, far from it again. (applause, laughter) Nor, and this is a pretty strong statement, do I believe in all that theologians advocate. That's a pretty big one, isn't it, for a small fellow like me.

I agree wholeheartedly that unemployment is the most important thing facing not only Canada, but the whole Western world. I agree with that 100 per cent. You'll get no argument from me there. But, as a man who dabbles a little bit in politics, I have to say there has to be a reason for unemployment. There are two main reasons for unemployment, in my estimation.

The first is mechanization. Mechanization does cause unemployment. Some people will disagree with me on that. I don't think mechanization is a very important explanation for unemployment. Instead, I think that a depressed economy is the real reason for unemployment -- a depressed economy. All we have to do is look at the nations of the world. Where there is a buoyant economy, unemployment immediately decreases. My point, therefore, is this. When interest rates jump to 22½ per cent, here is what happens. First we get a depressed economy, then we have wholesale bankruptcy, and with bankruptcy comes unemployment. We increased unemployment by around 600,000 people when interest rates went up in Canada.

JOSEPH GAVIN, CHAIRMAN: Perhaps you could direct yourself to a specific question or....

SPEAKER #21: The specific question is this. It is addressed to all panelists. Is it morally right to charge any interest rate that you can get away with? I want all panelists to answer.

JOSEPH GAVIN, CHAIRMAN: Thank you.

ISIDORE GORSKI: No, that would be usury. The church and the Scriptures have always stood against usury as a principle. We need to talk about what is usurous, perhaps, but to charge any interest rate you want, with no control whatsoever, has never been advocated by the church. I speak as a theologian, not an economist.

REX BODA: At one time the church was very strong in its condemnation of usury. But then the whole view of money changed. There was a shift from the original position. I think the church would be very much opposed to excessive interest-taking, but to define when interest becomes excessive could be a problem. Yes, at one time the church was against usury. But right now interest-taking in itself is not considered immoral by the church. However, I would say that charging interest in an excessive way, of course, enters the moral sphere. But what that precise line is, I don't know.

JAMES SCHALL: I only have one brief comment. When you start talking about unemployment without talking about what causes employment, you are talking about a kind of economic abstraction. Of course, we cannot deny that there are real people unemployed and that there are real problems connected with this, and that a civil society needs some way to handle this. But it's never going to do us any good whatsoever to complain about unemployment unless we concern ourselves with the <u>causes</u> of employment. Is there any relationship between our abstractions about the causes and the real cause of unemployment? We must redefine and change our attitudes towards work, interest, innovation, newness, change, and entrepreneurship. Until we do our concern about unemployment is all but irrelevent. We must realize that an economy requires innovation, etc. Unless we have insight into what does create wealth, we are never going to solve the problem of unemployment. Wealth ought to be created, it seems to me, and it is very important to stress this.

JOSEPH GAVIN, CHAIRMAN: Dr. Block. Very briefly.

WALTER BLOCK: That's impossible, but I'll do my best....

JOSEPH GAVIN, CHAIRMAN: There are several yet to ask questions. Continue.

WALTER BLOCK: I agree that the employment question is crucial. I have tried to outline one major cause of unemployment, namely the minimum wage law. I did so because the minimum wage law has been advocated by unions and a greater role for unions has been called for by the Canadian Conference of Catholic Bishops. So, I can't agree that all the bishops are doing is calling attention to the morality and the social and human aspects of unemployment. I say, on the contrary, that they are proposing technical solutions to unemployment. Namely, a stronger minimum wage law. But this would cause more unemployment; it would worsen their problem, not solve it.

The statement has been made that employment is too important to be left to markets. This is like saying that polio is too important to be left to the Salk vaccine. The Salk vaccine is the cure for polio; markets, namely, the eradication of minimum wage laws, are the cure for unemployment.

Now, on to usury. Usury laws, which forbid or limit people as to the interest rates they can charge, are a direct attack on the preferential option for the poor. Because it is the poor that are singled out for harm by usury laws. First of all, usury laws lower the amount of loanable funds that come onto the market and as we know, the poor have the least amount of collateral. So if there are fewer loanable funds, the poor will be the first ones turned away. When we have usury laws, the science of economics teaches us that the poor are the first ones to get cut off. As a result, the poor have to go to blackmarket loan sharks where they pay treble and quadruple interest rates. So, usury laws are an attack on the poor. They violate the preferential option for the poor espoused by the bishops.

SPEAKER #22: I'm from Plenty, Saskatchewan, and I would like to direct this comment and question to Walter Block. This afternoon Mr. Block made reference to the Fraser Institute's opposition to rent controls. He said that rent controls are not in the public interest. I had assumed that somewhere along the line during his presentation that he would have set out the rationale for that statement. I wonder if we could have a brief explanation of that now, and then I would like to respond to it.

WALTER BLOCK: Bless you. Bless you. That's just what I want to do. (laughter)

While I am on this topic, I feel I must reply to the man who took me up on the Gunnar Myrdal quote. But first, let me answer your question. Rent control is like placing a stop sign in front of the investor, or at least a yellow light, and telling him that if you invest your money in one particular area, namely residential rental units, it will be subject to controls. Whereas, if you invest your money in any other area, wristwatches, glasses, auditoriums, ties, what have you, your investment will not be subject to the red tape, to the onerous controls.

So what do you think is the effect of rent control? It is, of course, to divert resources that would otherwise be invested in residential housing, to any other area of endeavour, for example, commercial real estate. It's no accident that in cities that have rent control for residential areas but not for commercial, you'll see cranes, large buildings going up -- but none or very few of them are residential.

I would say that if we had rent control for commercial property but not for residential, the process would be inverted. Instead of having building in the commercial area, in hotels and office buildings, there would be residential construction, not commercial.

So the point is that rent control is a way of diverting resources away from precisely where poor tenants need them. If you really wanted to help poor tenants, the thing to do -- this is a big secret -- is to control everything else under the sun except residential rental units. So bad is rent control as a means of helping poor tenants. Because if you controlled everything else, then people who would have invested their money in these other things will now invest their money in residential rental units. And as we know, the greater the supply of residential rental units, the lower the rents, which is what we want. So how can rent control help if the very opposite of rent control is proven to be in the interest of the people?

Now, let me read and review the quotation from Gunnar Myrdal. Gunnar Myrdal says, "Rent control has in certain Western countries constituted maybe the worst example of poor planning by governments lacking courage and vision." Here is a similar quote from Assar Lindbeck, another Socialist economist, "In many cases rent control appears to be the most efficient technique presently known to destroy a city, except for bombing." I was quoting these eminent leftists to indicate that the economics profession is virtually united on the question of rent control. Rent control is not the best way to help poor tenants, indeed, it does the very opposite.

But, the objector from the audience said, well, the reason Gunnar Myrdal opposed rent control is different than the reason the Fraser Institute did. This happens to be false. Myrdal opposed it for the same reason, namely that it diverts resources from where they are most needed. And then the man said something that was true. Namely that Gunnar Myrdal favours housing subsidies. But of what relevance is that? Gunnar Myrdal has views on hundreds of other things too. The point is, this is a denial of the scientific method. The scientific method insists on what in economics is called ceterus paribus, or holding all other things constant. That is, we can only deal with one problem at a time. The question before us, at least I thought so when I edited this book, <u>Rent Control: Myths and Realities</u>, is, "what are the effects of rent control?" Not "what are the effects of everything else under the sun." We have other books on other proposals, like housing subsidies, which is a very different question. But on the question of rent control, the evidence is clear, the theory is clear. Rent control doesn't help tenants. Anyone who attacks the Fraser Institute on this is not helping the poor of Canada. Nor is he acting in accordance with what the bishops are advocating, the preferential option for the poor.

JOSEPH GAVIN, CHAIRMAN: This gentleman here.

SPEAKER #22: I asked to be able to respond, Mr. Chairperson.

JOSEPH GAVIN, CHAIRMAN: Oh, I beg your pardon.

SPEAKER #22: I have the privilege to work in an area of social and co-operative housing. And I do so from a Christian perspective. It was our experience in that situation that this utopian scheme you advocate, Dr. Block, has not happened yet and likely will never happen. Therefore, in order to protect persons who are oppressed by the systems and the structures of our economic society, rent controls are necessary. They give human dignity to families and persons. That's the other side of the coin.

SPEAKER #23: I'm from Regina. I'm a member of the general board of the Christian Church Disciples of Christ for Canada and the United States, although I am not a minister.

We have heard considerable talk today about the question of justice from the point of view of the rights of the people. But I have been disappointed that we haven't heard much from the perspective of obligations. This question will be for Dr. Block, by the way.

Economists tell us that money is a medium of exchange. But this only says that it conveys the right to control the output of labour. And it fails to address the question of responsibility for the application of labour. Now, in the present crisis we see two things. One is that our economic system is inherently unsuitable for a period of zero growth. But secondly, we lack investment. We lack investment because people who have money have not invested it in ways which tend to keep the business cycle in operation. My question then is, in what way and in what degree does the privilege in the form of wealth carry an obligation?

WALTER BLOCK: In what way does wealth carry an obligation? I don't think that wealth carries any obligation with it whatsoever...

SPEAKER #23: That's what I was afraid of. (laughter)

WALTER BLOCK: ...that is not held by people with less wealth. I think that people have rights and obligations based on their humanity. That's the source from which rights and obligations derive. Rights and obligations do not derive from the amount of wealth we have, or the amount of intelligence we have, or the amount of effort we put out, or any other criteria apart from our humanity.

I think that behind this question lies an economic fallacy. The economic fallacy is that the reason people get rich is because other people become impoverished. The way to gain wealth is by pushing other people down, in this view. In certain epochs of our history, especially during biblical times, this was roughly true. As Father Sadowsky mentioned before, the path towards wealth was the political means, namely stealing, in effect. Whether it was legal or illegal theft, it was grabbing other people's possessions and keeping them for yourself. That is how many people became wealthy. In those days, people felt that the economic pie always had to remain the same size. The way one got richer was by grabbing the other person's slice. So he had less.

Nowadays, thank goodness, we have another path toward wealth, the economic means -- that is, the creation of wealth out of nothing but our entrepreneurial insights and the sweat of our brow. The pie gets bigger, in other words. That's how wealth occurs nowadays. So I think if there is any obligation of wealth, and there isn't, it is to get richer. Because the way you get richer, the result of your becoming richer, is to enrich everyone else. Henry Ford, for example, got fabulously rich.

The way he did so was by enriching other people in society. He made it possible for the first time, for poor and middle-class persons to be able to afford to buy an automobile. Beforehand, automobiles were playthings of the rich, the very rich. Ford got rich by uplifting everyone else. He did not get rich by pushing people down.

SPEAKER #23: Can I make a short comment?

JOSEPH GAVIN, CHAIRMAN: Yes.

SPEAKER #23: The biblical teaching says, "To whom much is given from them much shall be expected."

JOSEPH GAVIN, CHAIRMAN: Would you care to identify yourself, please.

SPEAKER #24: I'm a peace activist from Regina. I think what we have largely been subjected to this afternoon and evening is a kind of Reaganomics without Reagan's foreign and military policy. And I would like to say, that everything we do, we do in the context of a world with over 50,000 nuclear weapons; a world with more tonnage of weaponry per person than there is food. How can we discuss theology, Third World development and economic justice without considering the increased use of military force in defence of economic inter-ests? I'll give an example: the use of cruise missiles. The battleship New Jersey was brought out of mothballs this year to be refitted with Tomahawk cruise missiles. It sat off Nicaragua earlier this year and then Lebanon. The cruise missile is being used like a gun during a bank robbery. It has not actually fired -- yet -- but it is being held to somebody's head.

There is also the violence of the internal repression and death squads which brutally fought the fulfillment of the aspirations of people in so many countries. I can think immediately of countries in Central America. I am sure other people can furnish lots of other examples. How can we conduct this so-called dialogue without addressing the increasing repression and suppression of dissent? This is even part of the increasing militarization of our own society here in Canada.

Perhaps people don't realize that an increasing proportion of the defence budget in Canada is being allocated to internal repression of dissent. By coincidence, I have recently been reading a book on war and peace. It is about historians and the way they have justified the cold war, to put it very bluntly. It could have been written yesterday and it could have been written about economists. My final question: is the hidden agenda of the Fraser Institute to open up Saskatchewan for high tech industries with military applications?

JOSEPH GAVIN, CHAIRMAN: Dr. Block, would you like to reply?

WALTER BLOCK: First of all I would like to know what happened to the money I paid this lady to ask me about women's questions? I was dying to answer that one, and I can't. But I hope someone else will ask me about the fact that women get paid less than men.

Let me talk about Reaganomics instead, then. First of all, we are not the only ones who stick to economics. The topic of this panel is Ethical Reflections on the Economic Crisis. The bishops, themselves, wrote only on economics. They didn't talk about cruise missiles in their document. There is a division of labour. We can't possibly discuss every question every day. Surely economic problems, the unemployment crisis, is a crisis. Surely we can devote some of our time to that without being beaten over the head for not discussing other problems.

I also can't see how it can be said that this panel represents the Fraser Institute. We have tried and strived mightily to have a balance of opinion from all sides of the political spectrum.

SPEAKER #24: Could I just briefly reply?

JOSEPH GAVIN, CHAIRMAN: Very briefly, please.

SPEAKER #24: I am a graduate of the London School of Economics. It is my understanding of economics -- though perhaps superficial -- that one of the reasons we have so much unemployment is because of the recession, created by large amounts of government spending on weaponry which pushes up interest rates.

ISIDORE GORSKI: I just might mention to Dr. Block that the American bishops have written a very powerful pastoral letter on the whole question of nuclear disarmament and I suspect the Canadian bishops will soon follow suit.   That particular letter has caused a great deal of debate and also a great deal of opposition, particularly from groups much like the Fraser Institute.

SPEAKER #25: I am the man from outer space. (laughter) I say that because you may find my next question rather hard to understand. I must say that I am rather disappointed with the discussion today. The major topic, which is central to what we are supposed to be discussing here, hasn't really been brought up by anybody. We have sort of touched around it.

What I am referring to is the use of coercion and violence in the economic situation. There are two ways that people can deal with one another. They can either deal in a voluntary, cooperative manner or they can use, or threaten to use, violence. Those are the only two ways possible for people to deal with one another. By definition, transactions which are cooperative and voluntary belong to the market. We are talking about willing sellers and willing buyers -- people who voluntarily enter into transactions. By definition, everything else falls into the involuntary or the coercive category.

What people aren't talking about here is, how does that operate?   How big a component does that make in our transactions? I'll say that it makes quite a large impact on the market, on those voluntary transactions. Now, everybody here who has talked about the market being modified in some way or other, has really couched their remarks in the language of voluntary giving. People should be willing to share wealth. He bestows upon the owner the responsibility to share his wealth. All that is well and good. If it is voluntary, it fits into the market side of transactions. No one can dispute that.

JOSEPH GAVIN, CHAIRMAN: Do you think you could come to the point.

SPEAKER #25: Yes, I can. What I am talking about is the widepsread use, and I might add the illegitimate use, of law to force people to do things they wouldn't otherwise choose to do. The moral question which I think is very pertinent and central here is -- how do people who want to see good things done for humanity justify the use of, or the threat of the use of, violence to accomplish their ends? I would like to ask this of the four panelists up there and I would like everybody in the audience to ask it of themselves.

JOSEPH GAVIN, CHAIRMAN: Would the panel like to answer that?

REX BODA: Are you an anarchist? Are you an anarchist yourself? Do you believe in the existence of civil society?

SPEAKER #25: I believe in a society where no one has the legitimate right to commit robbery or murder.

REX BODA: What about the legitimate obligation of the police to stop him? Is that...

SPEAKER #25: Absolutely. People have the right to defend themselves.

REX BODA: You're not an anarchist? So that therefore you do believe yourself in some sort of power in society?

SPEAKER #25: No, I believe in the right of people to defend themselves against the illegitimate use, the aggressive use of coercion...

REX BODA: You do believe there is such a thing as legitimate coercion?

SPEAKER #25: There is defensive violence which might be employed or non-violent defence and there is aggression.

JOSEPH GAVIN, CHAIRMAN: Would you precisely re-phrase your question?

SPEAKER #25: My question is this. What is so moral about committing violence or threatening to commit violence to do good works? That's my question.

REX BODA: Well, there is nothing moral about it. And yet that is exactly what we do when we tell the landlord that he can't rent his building for a fair market price, that he has to rent it at some other price. The option he has is either to knuckle under and rent it for the controlled price or have his property confiscated, through fines. Perhaps he will lose his building or he might even be thrown in jail.

It is appropriate for society through discussion and debate in legislatures and so forth and various other pressures that might be brought to bear, to set down guidelines that will regulate the society. We must expect people to live within these rules. That is a responsibility of all citizens: to enter into that process and establish the rules and guidelines we live by. And I don't see that as violence or coercion. It is in accordance with logic and reason. That is quite appropriate. Society couldn't function otherwise. It would be anarchy.

SPEAKER #25: Are you suggesting that the majority has the right to do whatever it wishes to the minority, as long as it's got through due process of legislation and law?

REX BODA: I guess you would have to go back to some basic understanding of what is just and what is right. And it would be the responsibility of the majority not to violate those basic understandings. As a theologian, I see the basic understandings of justice in terms of revelation itself, and in the character of God. I am limited by that. I would therefore be careful not to force a capricious view on the minority.

SPEAKER #25: Well, can you be more specific about how you define what minority rights are?

JOSEPH GAVIN, CHAIRMAN: I think you have had fair time at the microphone. Other people have been waiting for some time. I think we should move on now.

SPEAKER #26: I am a grain farmer. I would like to ask a question. Two of the panelists used the term "productivity." They spoke as if productivity had some direct relationship to income or earning capacities. But what is defined as productivity is entirely different for different people. I would define productivity in terms of creating foodstuffs. I am sure that some of the panelists would include as productive some of the sales persons who attempt to sell me commodities to run my farm. In most cases those sales persons are just in my road. (laughter) They don't give me the information I need on the purchase. And yet because they have some kind of power behind them, they will earn a large income. I don't see the productivity there. I wouldn't call that productivity, even though in your scheme of things it is considered productivity. That is my first point.

As a grain farmer, I am interested in ethics in terms of Third World development. Because of the way the system operates, and the way I am caught up in it, I find it very difficult to feel good about producing wheat which then gets hard-peddled to Brazil. For I understand that this results not in feeding the poor in Brazil, but in taking the land away from the people who produce for themselves so that they can produce a cash crop to buy my wheat. That is an ethical dilemma for me. Under the present economic system there is no way around that. There is no solution if I am going to survive under the system where the economy determines who survives and who does not. But the Gospel reverses this scenario. It puts the people first. In this view, we must first find out from those who are now producing their own food, what can benefit them in trade, and what can benefit me at this end. If these Third World peoples are the ones given the power to determine the economic system, then I think it is ethical. I do not feel it is ethical now.

JAMES SCHALL: I just want to make one brief point. There is a great variety of productivity. You say we have got to have a productive society, and then you mention the fact that it means one thing for the man who produces grain and it means another, for example, for a man like Father Gavin who is the President of Campion College. As well, it means another thing for a painter. Yes, productivity is very heterogeneous. That is to say the creation of new wealth takes place in a wide variety of areas. This is what civilization is all about.

I would caution you on one thing, though. We all live in imperfect societies to some degree. The fact that there are many kinds of serious problems in any existing society is part of the human condition. Aristotle himself said there is a distinction between good societies and bad societies; and within good societies there is a distinction between good, better and best societies; in bad societies there is a distinction between the not-so-bad, the bad and the really awful. Throughout the world there is a wide variety of relatively good and bad kinds of societies. We are unsettled about ours, in comparison to others. This may be good or may be not so good. But we ought not put our whole intellectual, religious and moral effort behind the notion that the creation of an absolutely perfect society is possible. It seems to me that that kind of an idea, or subconscious pre-supposition, is very unsettling. It is perhaps, even, a dangerous position. There has got to be some point at which, while not being necessarily content with what is not so very good, we recognize the difficult and the practical problems connected with making something better. It seems to me that there is a certain spiritual problem which applies to many people, particularly religious people, regarding the question of productivity.

WALTER BLOCK: I should like to address the topic of Third World development, trade, tariffs and self-sufficiency. As far as I am concerned, the main impediment to Third World development is the vicious, immoral and depraved tariffs that Canada and other Western developed countries place on the importation of goods from the impoverished Third World.

For example, Canadians can produce wheat a lot more efficiently than can the people in the Third World, and these nations can produce shoes a lot cheaper than us. In an ideal, or even in a better society, we could be trading our wheat for their shoes. If so, both parties to the trade could benefit, especially the poor. We could be dragging them up from the degradation of poverty in which they now unfortunately exist. Instead, our Canadian government, for various reasons too complex to mention here, has made this all but impossible. We have set up tariff and other trade barriers so that the poor people in the Third World can't export their shoes to us. As a result, they lose jobs and they lose productivity. We have to pay $30, $40 and $50 for these shoes which we could be importing from the Third World for $2 or $5 or $10 -- so the poor in Canada also lose.

I am very much in sympathy with this gentleman's question. We have so many barriers to trade. We have wheat marketing boards which interfere with his God-given rights to grow wheat. We have tariffs which stop him trading that wheat for the shoes of a poor man in the Third World. And yet the bishops, whose paper we are discussing at this conference, on this panel particularly, have come out in favour of self-sufficiency. That is, they have come out in favour of tariffs and other trade barriers, in effect. I think this is a tragedy. It is a violation of the preferential option of the poor. It is a way of consigning the Third World to the degradation squalor, and poverty from which they now suffer.

SPEAKER #27: I'm in the Department of Political Science at this university.

My question is mostly addressed to Dr. Block but it pertains also to some of the observations of Father Gorski. I think that Dr. Block's comments today illustrate very well a fundamental philosophical difference we have seen at this conference; namely, between those who emphasize their belief that we still have a fairly open, free, competitive economy, and those who believe that the economy is much more concentrated in the hands of a relatively few powerful corporations and individuals.

My specific question is, what guarantees are there that if we were to do away with the minimum wage, the large corporations and powerful individuals would not hold down people's wages. Dr. Block used the analogy of Horatio Alger and the babysitter. To me, personally, this seems quite remote from the kind of critical economy which we see today in advanced industrial countries. As I have indicated, it seems to be much more concentrated in relatively few hands. Here is where my idea relates to what Father Gorski said dealing with his emphasis on labour as opposed to capital. Contrary to Dr. Block, the minimum wage is needed to protect labour against the possible manipulations, whether formal or informal, of capital. I am interested in the replies of both Drs. Block and Gorski.

ISIDORE GORSKI: First of all I want to say that I have carefully gone through the bishops' paper; not only do they not favour the minimum wage law, they don't even mention it. Nor is there any explicit defense of tariffs. I must therefore conclude that Dr. Block takes their fifth strategy and reads something into it which isn't there. If I may remind us, it is in the fifth strategy that the bishops call for the labour unions to play a much more decisive and responsible role in developing strategies for economic recovery and employment. That fifth strategy doesn't say anything about the minimum wage.

Now to the point I want to make in answer to Dr. Block; to my mind, the real need for a minimum wage is to protect precisely against the exploitation which results from the corporations. Perhaps the minimum wage level in certain areas might be too high. But I am definitely in favour of a minimum wage in order to protect against that exploitation which historically has been part of the economic scene.

WALTER BLOCK: The reason I mentioned the minimum wage is because the bishops state that their goal is twofold: one, to solve unemployment and two, to help the least, the last and the lost among us -- the most downtrodden, the people at the bottom of the economic pyramid. So I ask, well, what causes the unemployment among the lowest and the least skilled workers? And my answer is -- the minimum wage law. Of course, the bishops never mentioned it. That is the problem. They don't mention the minimum wage law at all. This is almost an irresponsible lack on their part, in the paper. If they are truly concerned with poverty and unemployment, and specifically with the unemployment of the worst-off amongst us, they have to mention the minimum wage law. But they don't. Instead, they call upon labour unions to play a greater role. This is like asking the fox to come in and help guard the chickens. The biggest part of organized labour's plank, one of their staunchest held convictions, is the importance of the minimum wage law.

Let us now talk about the second principle of the bishops. There are two principles in this document. One, with which I have agreed, is the preferential option for the poor. But there is another one. And that is the priority of labour over capital.

Consider the following case. Wayne Gretzky is a labourer, a very rich labourer. There are widows with small houses who rent out rooms to tenants. They are capitalists. They are very poor. The point is, if there is a conflict between a rich labourer and a poor capitalist, reliance on principle 1 gives us one answer, but principle 2 gives another answer -- the diametric opposite. I deduce that the two principles are inconsistent. I like and admire the first principle, the preferential option for the poor. The second one is just Marxism.

How so? Marx held a view called the labour theory of value, in accordance with which labour was responsible for the value of products. That is, a product had value to the extent, and only to the extent, that it embodied the efforts of workers. And if labour did not receive the full product; namely, if there was anything left over for interest or profit or what have you, this was exploitation of labour. But a moment's thought will convince us that labour does not create all value. If you pick up a gold nugget, it is worth a lot of money but there is little or no labour involved. In contrast you can labour for years and make a big mud pie and it is still worth nothing.

The point about the minimum wage law being needed to protect poor people is the very opposite of the truth. The minimum wage law doesn't protect people. The minimum wage causes them to be unemployed. It consigns them to a life of idleness. It thus promotes drunkenness, crime and other such evils. It is much better to earn $1 an hour and have a job where you can learn skills and increase your productivity, than it is to be forced into idleness at $4 per hour.

SPEAKER #28: Mr. Chairman, I would like to use the podium. May I?

JOSEPH GAVIN, CHAIRMAN: Please be very brief, then.

SPEAKER #28: The reason I need to read is because I wear contact lenses and I am having difficulty reading down there.

JOSEPH GAVIN, CHAIRMAN: All right.

SPEAKER #28: It seems to me we are missing the key point here. The real problem is, how is wealth created? We can't create wealth by legislating that there must be a job. It has to be a God-given wealth that is given to man for nothing. But all we have been dealing with here is the difference between what my labour versus your labour is worth, in simple fact.

Wealth originates from all raw materials. Industries generate wealth at a ratio of $1/$5. For every dollar you give industry for the finished product, it becomes $5. Agriculture is different. Agriculture consumes 40 per cent of its own product thereby generating $7 of earned income for every $1 that is paid into it.

Unfortunately, we have exploited agriculture to the point where we are paying it less than 2 per cent of the national income, when it requires 7 per cent to generate the wealth.

JOSEPH GAVIN, CHAIRMAN: Excuse me. Would you please come to a point?

SPEAKER #28: Yes, I'm going to. And it is in this way that money is related to all of our problems. We have to address the question -- how are we going to distribute wealth without paying agriculture its just wage? This relates agriculture back to the minimum wage law. Farm workers today are being paid less than minimum wage. If we don't restore agriculture in balance with other sectors, as was mentioned before, we will be faced with a worse depression than we had in the 1930s.

JOSEPH GAVIN, CHAIRMAN: All right. Thank you.

ISIDORE GORSKI: I am four-square for a good deal of government intervention. I strongly favour government interference in the economy, and so again I take issue with Dr. Block. I still insist on the priority of labour. We must have more labour-intensive rather than capital-intensive investment. And here I might refer to the encyclical written by Pope John Paul II. But again I wish to add caution here. There are a lot of solutions which have to be debated and discussed. The answers do not come easily. But at least we should sit down and try to work these out together in a situation of dialogue between big business, the labour unions, the state, and the church.

JOSEPH GAVIN, CHAIRMAN: Next speaker, please.

SPEAKER #29: I'm a teacher here on campus. Before this conference, I didn't know anything about the Fraser Institute. When that little brochure* came across my desk, I thought it was wonderful. At last the university is going to start talking about something that's terribly important, theology. And so I registered and I even made a donation. I've now heard some representatives of the Fraser Institute. I hope I'm not over-simplifying, but it seems to me it was said that there were conference rules and that one should obey them. And I also heard somebody trying to say that Jesus said, "love your neighbour as yourself." I heard someone else say that foreign aid was ill-conceived, that you ought not to give such aid. I also heard somebody say that Jesus said, "give a cup of cold water in His name." I have now been listening to the idea of getting rid of the minimum wage.

I thought I was coming here to hear a central focus on God, on theos, not on productivity and the market. And I also expected that if we were centring our discussion on theos we would also be focusing on those who are made in the image of God, the person. And so my question goes to Dr. Block. You want to get rid of the minimum wage; what do you make, then, of Jesus's parable of hiring in the vineyard, where He paid the same wage to those who came for the last hour?

----

* See Appendix B. -- Editors

WALTER BLOCK: I would like to answer, but I am mindful that I might have taken up more than my fair share of the microphone so far. In view of that, I have no comment.

JOSEPH GAVIN, CHAIRMAN: Do any of the other panel members want to say something. Order please.

JAMES SCHALL: Let me make a brief comment on that. That particular parable is a parable and not necessarily a lesson in economic doctrine. And the parable can be interpreted in several ways. I realize that you are probably skeptical about the notion of interpreting parables. However, I would caution you as follows. That parable doesn't bear on the question of whether anybody was paid a legitimate wage or not. The first man was paid a legitimate wage according to the parable itself, and the man was doing a just thing throughout. The only one who made an accusation of injustice, as I recall, was the person to whom more was given than what the first man received.

Let us return to our minimum wage example. Let's suppose you work for, oh, I don't know; let's suppose you work for Campion College. I understand that it is very difficult to work there. (laughter) But let's suppose you work there for minimum wage and the President has agreed to pay you this minimum wage according to his conscience and the finances of the university. And so you work for that much, and he pays you at the end of the day. If the minimum wage is $4 per hour, and you work hard for eight hours, then you earn $32 a day.

As it so happens you find out that in his large heart Father Gavin has also hired somebody who starts at 11 o'clock A.M. and pays that person the same $32. The question is, are you being cheated? You start at 8:00 A.M., the other person at 11:00 A.M. You both finish at 5:00 P.M., and receive equal pay. Have you been cheated? That is the question the parable addresses. It is quite conceivable that the second person's remuneration was not necessarily just. But this doesn't violate the first person's contract, or reduce his wage, and it doesn't necessarily violate the second person's rights. That is my answer to that question.

JOSEPH GAVIN, CHAIRMAN: We are past the deadline but there are three other questioners so we will have to limit ourselves to them.

SPEAKER #30: I am a retired person. I was on active service during World War II. What I know about the civil economy, I have read. This question is to Dr. Block. There was a time when a lot of the labour force were in uniform and a lot more of the labour force were working in defence establishments. Resources with which houses were built were also being used for the war effort. In that context, there were many marriages and a lot of family formation because marriages had been postponed during the depression, and soldiers had money and they were getting married right and left and setting up housekeeping and needed accommodation. So my question is: is rent control ever justified?

WALTER BLOCK: What I said before I meant in all sincerity. I was afraid that I was taking up too much time and that it was unfair. I don't want to do that. If the chair will recognize me, I would be happy to answer that question, otherwise I will give another "no comment."

JOSEPH GAVIN, CHAIRMAN: The question was addressed to you.

WALTER BLOCK: Rent control can be justified, but certainly not on moral grounds. I think it is never justified on moral grounds because it is equivalent to theft. It is the theft of the person's property who is trying to rent the apartment. But rent control certainly is justified on pragmatic grounds -- if your purpose is to entice resources away from residential rental housing. That is the effect of rent control: to retard the creation of new housing. If that is your purpose, then you are pragmatically justified in enacting rent control.

SPEAKER #31: I'm a retired union negotiator. Just in the last two months I completed 11 years as a human rights commissioner in the province of Saskatchewan and I am still doing work on occupational health and safety and as an injured workers' consultant regarding workers' compensation.

I want to deal with the question of minimum wage legislation. I see a contradiction and I have to go back to my experience in the early 1930s. Then I gave evidence in the Province of British Columbia, City of Vancouver, to a committee that was set up by the government to examine the minimum wage. At that time it was $5.25 a week, for a 44 hour week, and I was asked whether it should be increased. The Fraser Institute might well look up the report of the late Magistrate Jamieson and Lady Rex Eaton. Both these women recommended that the minimum wage level be increased to $6.50, for a 44 hour week. But this was rejected by the government of the day. I remember being unemployed for a great deal of the 1930s, and I didn't notice that keeping the minimum wage down did a darn thing for employment. But this is contradictory to Dr. Block's remarks on the subject.

Henry Ford was praised for investing money and paying $1 an hour. That was $1 an hour when the minimum wage in the area was $7.00 a week for a 44 hour week. And he wasn't paying that to high-skilled people. He was paying it to the unskilled workers on the assembly line. So if Ford was so helpful, as Dr. Block has said he was, how could refusing to raise the minimum wage to a little over $6 a week be harmful? I can't reconcile the kinds of arguments that go back and forth on this question. The minimum wage has but very little effect, except that it means that nobody can go below a rock bottom point. Whether it is the least-skilled worker or not, surely with today's prices, there isn't a minimum wage across this country that is exorbitant in those terms.

By the way, in the 1930s, we had poor provinces that never even had a minimum wage and they still had unemployment, so I don't know where his argument comes from.

JOSEPH GAVIN, CHAIRMAN: I have to ask you to be more brief.

SPEAKER #31: I will. Take the question of equal pay. In my 11 years on the Human Rights Commission, we had the chore of adjudicating complaints about equal pay, conducting hearings and making awards. It is simply not correct to argue that the jobs women take pay less because those are the kind of jobs they are. One adjudication we made was at the branch of one of the largest steel companies on this earth. They had a woman working at a higher level of skill than the four men she was compared with, and they didn't pay her as much as them. Finally, in the University of Regina, we adjudicated an equal pay case affecting roughly one hundred employees. We made an award and found that the women were indeed being underpaid.

JOSEPH GAVIN, CHAIRMAN: Thank you very much. Did you wish to comment?

WALTER BLOCK: I am very happy to have the opportunity to answer the question. There are really two questions. One is about the minimum wage and the other about equal pay for equal work and discrimination against women and why it is that women earn less than men.

I will briefly refer to the minimum wage. Since I have already discussed it, let me just focus on the point that there were four provinces that didn't have a minimum wage and yet had unemployment. My view on this is that the minimum wage is a sufficient condition for unemployment, but not a necessary condition. (A) is a sufficient condition for (B) if and only if (B) appears when (A) appears -- which means, if you have a minimum wage, then you will have unemployment. But it is not a necessary condition. That is, you can have the (B) without the (A). You can have unemployment without the minimum wage law, because there are other causes of unemployment besides the minimum wage law.

I have been anxious to answer the question of women's wages all day, ever since the first panel, when it was mentioned. The Fraser Institute has published a book called Discrimination, Affirmative Action and Equal Opportunity. In that book we made an exhaustive and intensive study of both racial and sexual discrimination. Let's forget about racial discrimination for the moment and only consider sexual discrimination.

Our findings attempted to unearth the cause of women earning some 60 per cent of what men earn, on average. A major cause is the asymmetrical effects of marriage on male and female incomes. That is to say, marriage as an institution enhances male income and reduces female income. The reason for this, whether we like it or not, is that women do a disproportionate share of housework, a disproportionately high share of the child rearing and in many other ways act so as to maximize the male income and not the female. This is despite the best efforts of feminists to achieve more equitable sharing of housework and baby care.

For example, there might be two chemists, a man and his wife. If the women does more work with the children and more housework, that is one explanation for unequal wages. If she got married very young and had these children and never got her Ph.D. in order that the husband could do this, that's another reason. Now suppose she has her Ph.D. but an offer comes in some far away city. If it's for the husband (which means she'll just have to take any job she can get there), research shows that the family is much more likely to take such a job than if the female, the wife, gets such a job offer and the male just has to tag along for whatever job he can land.

A little bit of statistics: I don't like to mention statistics too much but they are very important in this context. In order to test the hypothesis of the effects of marriage on earnings ratios, we separated male and female income by marital status. We know that the overall female to male wage ratio is about 60 per cent. But we separated the Canadian population into two sub-categories. One category has never been touched by the institution of marriage. The other category is anyone who was ever touched, however slightly, by the institution of marriage. That includes the married, divorced, widowed, and separated.

Now, let me give you some statistics that will really shock you. Do you know what the female/male wage rate ratio for the ever-married category was? It was something like 32 or 33 per cent. This shows that in the ever-married sector, women earn only about a third of what men do. But do you know what the ratio was for males and females who were never touched in any way, manner, shape or form, by the institution of marriage? It was an astounding 99.2 per cent! If you don't believe it, check the book. Check the statistics. Look at the footnotes. I cannot possibly over-emphasize the importance of this finding: 99.2 per cent.

SPEAKER #32: I'm just an interested citizen. I want to ask Dr. Block if I understood him correctly to say that he didn't believe anybody was worth $100 an hour?

WALTER BLOCK: No, I just said that very few people have that kind of productivity. This means that very few people can produce in one hour of effort, hour in and hour out, goods and services worth $100 per hour. That's a very high rate of productivity. There might be some few people who could do that, like Wayne Gretsky, top doctors, attorneys, etc.

SPEAKER #32: Could I just ask one other question, perhaps of the whole panel? Do you think that the fact that a considerable number of people in Canada earn $100,000 or $200,000 or get $100,000 or $200,000, and maybe even $500,000 a year, contributes to the fact that there isn't enough money to pay a liveable minimum wage to the others.

JOSEPH GAVIN, CHAIRMAN: All right. We'll start here.

REX BODA: I'm not sure, I'm not an economist. I suspect that it probably would be minimal enough not to have a dramatic effect, but I don't really know.

ISIDORE GORSKI: This is precisely an area where the government must intervene through the tax laws. This is a solution that the Canadian bishops might well support. Unfortunately, most of the solutions usually proposed, whether with regard to inflation, and/or unemployment, are usually at the expense of the poor and the needy. They oft-times give tax write-offs for the rich. So I would say that this is where government can properly pursue an equitable program.

JAMES SCHALL: I take another viewpoint on this. Let us carefully consider anyone capable of earning as much money as you mention. If you prevent him from doing this, by taking money away from him in various fashions such as were suggested, then you reduce the incentive for him to do the kind of work which commands that income level. But a person who is paid such a salary is likely to be in the kind of position where he can create jobs. It is likely to be a productivity-creating position. Were your suggestion implemented, he would most likely not produce the wealth which produces the jobs that create more wealth in the society. Further, if you take the money away from him and distribute it, it won't go very far because there is not really very much money in the whole society earned in this manner.

I would suggest you read quite an important book, entitled In Search of Excellence. This is a book about the nature of successful organizations. It is extremely important that we have successful business organizations. And this requires people who can manage and direct them. But that kind of talent is quite rare. Very often the difference between the creation of jobs, and wealth, and the failure to do so is precisely whether or not these geniuses of productivity, development and growth have the proper incentives. If they do, they can create something where it never existed before. We must consider at least the possibility that the creation of wealth is not necessarily done at the expense of the poor. Wealth production can create something that did not exist before, and it is extremely important that this idea be clear.

WALTER BLOCK: I would agree with Father Schall, but complain that he only tells half the story. I think there is much truth in what he is saying. But in my view, some high salaries or high profits are made at the expense of the poor, and others are not. James Schall fully explicated the case where the rich do not exploit the poor. And I agree with him on that.

But under certain circumstances, the answer is yes, the rich can exploit the poor in their attempt to gain wealth. Because the government, the agency which Father Gorski is relying on to put things right, is itself one of the greatest engines for transferring funds from poor to rich! Father Gorski would of course oppose this, and I would agree with him; however, it is the government, whose actions he and the Catholic bishops would enhance, which is responsible for this. The government is the agency which gives large-scale businesses very unfair competitive advantages. It grants bail-outs. We talk about welfare for the poor, but government subsidies to corporations are really welfare for the rich, the "corporate welfare bums." And this is big welfare, not just pennies or a few dollars. This is an unconscionable effect of common government practice. It's one that I oppose fully because it is a violation of the free market principles of liberty. Government gives billions of dollars to large-scale corporations, it helps them concentrate, it gives them favours, it gives them subsidies, it gives them protection from competitors, it gives them bail-outs -- all at the expense of poor people. Where do you think this tax money comes from, in great part: from the poor and the middle classes.

To summarize my answer: if the great wealth is earned in the marketplace then Father Schall's answer is entirely correct. As he says, it's because these rich people earn so much that the people at the bottom of the income scale are doing as well as they are. But, when the money is derived illegitimately, not as part of the marketplace, then the questioner is perfectly correct. The rich do drive down and exploit the poor people. This distinction is crucial.

If I could just make one statement not as a member of this panel but in my capacity as a co-sponsor of this event. I would just like to say that the fact that there are still so many people here on a Sunday night long after 9:00 p.m., in freezing Regina in December, indicates that we have had a successful conference. Even if you don't agree with my own views, I hope that you will agree that we have succeeded in putting on a conference that was a well-balanced effort to dialogue meaningfully on economics and theology. (applause)

JOSEPH GAVIN, CHAIRMAN: One last question.

SPEAKER #33: I want to ask Dr. Block a question about his theoretical idea of the employer paying $1 to the uneducated, untrained native or handicapped person. And my question is this. What likelihood is there that an employer, whose interest is in his wealth, as you stated, Dr. Block, will agree to begin to pay $4 to the employee? Will he not, for an unskilled job, rather fire the person, as Mr. Bumstead always threatens to fire Dagwood whenever he asks for a raise, and instead of paying $4, hire another unskilled person, also at $1 an hour?

JOSEPH GAVIN, CHAIRMAN: Thank you.

WALTER BLOCK: If the employer is forced to pay $4 an hour then the worker is not really much of a bargain. He can be fired easily, at any slight disagreement or whim. But if the person is being paid only $1 an hour and his productivity is slightly higher than $1 an hour, then this person is making profit for the employer. He will not be fired whimsically. If he is, there will be other employers eager to snap him up at the very low $1 per hour. This is why students and young people have employment difficulties. This is a college community. When summer comes it is so hard for these students to find jobs because you must pay them a certain minimum wage. If you could pay them $1 or $2 you would find, amazingly enough, that many more employers would be glad to hire them for jobs that do not exist at $4 an hour -- but would exist at $1 or $2 or $3 an hour.

SPEAKER #33: My concern is with the person who is earning the $1 for a long, long time. I know one refugee who is earning minimum wage or less, washing dishes. My concern is with that person who is fired...my concern is not how many other people there are to take that job. It is for that person who has lost his job because he is not being paid a decent wage. Just because, perhaps, they are less fortunate than you or me.

WALTER BLOCK: I would say the person to worry about is not the one who has succeeded in finding employment at the minimum wage level. He's on the ladder of employment. The person we should direct our attention toward is, as the bishops maintain, to the last, least and lost among us.

SPEAKER #33: That's who I am talking about.

WALTER BLOCK: Yes, namely, the person who is frozen off the employment ladder entirely. He is languishing in idleness. He is not learning anything. The person who has a job at least is earning and learning something. He has on-the-job training and hopefully one day he will increase his wages.

SPEAKER #33: It doesn't work that way. I'm afraid you are hopelessly naive. I think yours is an idle dream.

WALTER BLOCK: Well, we have differences of opinion.

JOSEPH GAVIN, CHAIRMAN: Thank you.

That is it, ladies and gentlemen. I would like to thank you, those of you who have stayed that extra half hour longer. I also thank the panelists, both these and the other two sets of panelists, for a stimulating conference. I would also like to say, on behalf of the University of Regina, Luther College and Campion College, that we were delighted that you turned out. Thank you very much for attending.

APPENDIX

A

UNIVERSITY OF REGINA

REGINA, CANADA S4S 0A2

OFFICE OF THE PRESIDENT

October 19, 1983.

Dear Sir/Madam:

This letter is an invitation for you to participate in a conference on "Theology, Third World Development, and Economic Justice," to be held at the University of Regina on Sunday, December 4, 1983, commencing at 1:30 p.m. The conference will be held in the Education Auditorium, Education Building.

The University of Regina, Campion College and Luther College are joining with the Centre for the Study of Economics and Religion, which is a division of the Fraser Institute of Vancouver, as co-sponsors of the conference. Several distinguished clerics and academicians have agreed to serve as panelists, and the conference promises to be a stimulating and thought-provoking experience.

I urge you to participate and request that you notify us as soon as possible of your intent to join us. We look forward to your response and your participation in this important event.

Yours sincerely,

Lloyd Barber,
President.

LB/bjs

B

THE CONFERENCE SPONSORS:

THE FRASER INSTITUTE,

THE UNIVERSITY OF REGINA,

CAMPION COLLEGE and

LUTHER COLLEGE

PRESENT:

THEOLOGY,
THIRD WORLD DEVELOPMENT
AND ECONOMIC JUSTICE

DECEMBER 4, 1983
University of Regina
Regina, Saskatchewan

Religious institutions have been taking a greater and greater role in the Canadian dialogue on economics, budgets, poverty, unemployment and other public policy issues. It is important that this contribution be based on the most professional analysis available, and on the keenest of moral and biblical insights. Accordingly, the sponsors of this conference have invited a selection of world renowned theologians, ethicists and economists, representative of all sides of the political spectrum, to discuss third world poverty, economic justice and unemployment. Provision has been made for extended interaction with attendees.

THE UNIVERSITY OF REGINA
The University of Regina is a growing community of more than 9,000 students and approximately 875 full-time faculty and staff.

More than half of our students are from areas outside the city of Regina. The University's development has always been closely associated with the growth and development of the province of Saskatchewan through a variety of programs and research areas.

CAMPION COLLEGE
Campion College is a co-educational university college federated with the University of Regina and has been directed by the Jesuit Fathers since its foundation in 1917. The college offers a liberal, humanistic education in the Arts and Science in an atmosphere that stresses the personal, the religious, the social, the cultural and the academic development of students.

LUTHER COLLEGE
Luther College is a college of the Evangelical Lutheran Church of Canada and is federated with the University of Regina. It offers its 400 students a quality liberal arts and science education, and the personalized attention and community atmosphere of a small christian college. In addition to its classes and student services, Luther offers residence accommodation to over 200 men and women.

THE FRASER INSTITUTE
The Centre for the Study of Economics and Religion, a division of the Fraser Institute, focuses attention on the interface between economics and religion through a series of seminars and publications. A tax exempt charitable organization, the Institute is located at 626 Bute Street, Vancouver, B.C. V6E 3M1. The Centre promotes dialogue amongst theologians and economists in order to further a better understanding of public issues.

DR. JUDITH A. ALEXANDER - Born in Australia, Dr. Alexander holds a Ph.D. from S.F.U. (Economics) and is presently Associate Professor and Head of the Department of Economics, University of Regina. She is published in *Canadian Public Policy, Canadian Journal of Economics*, the *Journal of Economic Theory, Commissioner*, and *Medical Care Insurance Commission of Saskatchewan*. A former member of the Board, Canadian Economics Association and University of Regina Faculty Association, Dr. Alexander is presently a member of Mr. Lalonde's Advisory Panel and Board Member of the Regina Symphony and the University Women's Club.

DR. TERRY ANDERSON - Professor of Christian Social Ethics, Vancouver School of Theology. Author of *The Ethics of Using Behaviour Mechanisms on Criminals, Ethics and Uranium Mining*, and *The Distribution of Authority in Health Care*. Fields of interest include The Theology and Ethics of Ecology, Feminism and Lands Claims of Native Peoples.

LORD PETER BAUER - Professor of Economics at the London School of Economics. He was recently elevated to the British House of Lords. An expert on Third World Economic Development, he is author of *Dissent on Development: Studies and Debates on Development Economics; Equality, the Third World and Economic Delusion; West African Trade: A Study of Competition; Oligopoly and Monopoly in a Changing Economy; Western Guilt and Third World Poverty*.

DR. WALTER BLOCK - Director, Centre for the Study of Economics and Religion; Senior Economist, The Fraser Institute. Author of *Amending the Combines Investigation Act*; and *Focus on Economics and the Canadian Bishops*. Editor of *Zoning: Its Cost and Relevance for the 1980s; Rent Control: Myths and Realities; Discrimination, Affirmative Action, and Equal Opportunity*.

DR. REX BODA - Dr. Boda is the President of Regina's Canadian Bible College/Canadian Theological Seminar. Prior to accepting his current position, Dr. Boda served on staff first as professor, then as academic dean. A graduate of Cornell University and Westminster Theological Seminary, Dr. Boda's primary areas of interest are theology and church history.

DR. JOSEPH B. GAVIN, S.J. - President of Campion College. He holds a Doctorate Degree in History in addition to degrees in Philosophy and Theology. Dr. Gavin's present research focuses on the Social Position of the Clergy in the Post Reformation English Church. Other areas of interest include the Reformation, the Renaissance and Nineteenth-Century Studies.

FATHER ISIDORE GORSKI - Professor of both Humanities and Religious Studies at Campion College. He holds degrees in Philosophy, Theology and Biblical Studies from the University of Toronto and Angelicum University and the Biblical Institute in Rome. Father Gorski gives classes in Old and New Testament literature as well as an

Introduction to Religion and a course on Jesus (In addition, Father Gorski teaches enquiry clas Catholic faith for the Archdiocese.

DR. PAUL HEYNE - Professor of Economics, University of Washington, Seattle; Ph.D. in Theology, University of Chicago. Author of *Private Keepers of the Public Interest* and of the best-selling college economics text, *The Economic Way of Thinking*.

PROF. DOUGLAS F. McARTHUR - Holds an undergraduate degree in Agriculture from the University of Saskatchewan and Masters degrees in Economics from Oxford and the University of Toronto. Presently Assistant Professor of Economics at the University of Regina. Formerly, Minister of Education, Deputy Minister of Agriculture and Deputy Minister of Northern Saskatchewan with the Saskatchewan Government. Currently researching and teaching in the fields of Public Sector Economics and Resource Economics.

DR. MURDITH MacLEAN - Presently Warden of St. John's College, University of Manitoba. An Anglican Priest (1964), with degrees in Philosophy from the University of Alberta, Birmingham (London), and Oxford. Holds a degree in Theology from St. John's College (Winnipeg) and has held teaching and administrative positions at the University of Alberta, Grand Prairie Regional College, Red Deer College and the University of Manitoba.

DR. ROLAND E. MILLER - Currently Professor of Islam and World Religions and Academic Dean of Luther College, University of Regina. Dr. Miller is holder of an M.Div. degree and has earned M.A. and Ph.D. degrees in Islamics, a field in which he has achieved an international reputation. His major book is a definitive study entitled *The Mappila Muslims of Kerala*. He is general editor of the William Carey Library Series on Islamics Studies and is presently Coordinator of the Religious Studies program of the University of Regina.

FATHER JAMES SADOWSKY, S.J. - Professor of Philosophy and Ethics, Fordham University, New York. Author of *Transubstantiation and Scholastic Philosophy; and Private Property and Collective Ownership*. Contributor to *The American Catholic Philosophical Review*.

FATHER JAMES SCHALL, S.J. - Professor of Government and Political Philosophy, Georgetown University. His recent books include *Liberation Theology in Latin America; The Distinctiveness of Christianity; The Church, the State, & Society in the Thought of John Paul II; Christianity & Politics*; and *Christianity & Life*.

DR. DONALD E. SHAW - Don Shaw is Vice President of the University of Regina where he served previously as Dean of the Faculty of Administration. He holds a Ph.D. in Economics and has served as a consultant to business and government. Dr. Shaw has publications in the areas of Social Responsibilities of Business.

THE PROGRAM

1:30-1:50 p.m. Registration & Coffee

1:50-2:00 p.m. Welcome Address: Walter Block

2:00-3:30 p.m. Panel #1
                LIBERATION THEOLOGY
                AND THIRD WORLD
                DEVELOPMENT

        Chairman: Dr. Donald E. Shaw

        Panelists: Lord Peter Bauer
                   Dr. Murdith MacLean
                   Prof. Douglas F. McArthur

3:30-3:45 p.m. Coffee Break

3:45-5:15 p.m. Panel #2
                RELIGION, EGALITARIANISM,
                AND ECONOMIC JUSTICE

        Chairman: Dr. Roland E. Miller

        Panelists: Dr. Judith A. Alexander
                   Dr. Terry Anderson
                   Dr. Paul Heyne
                   Father James Sadowsky, S.J.

5:15-7:00 p.m. Dinner Break

7:00-8:30 p.m. Panel #3
                ETHICAL REFLECTIONS ON
                THE ECONOMIC CRISIS

        Chairman: Dr. Joseph B. Gavin, S.J.

        Panelists: Dr. Walter Block
                   Dr. Rex Boda
                   Father Isidore Gorski
                   Father James Schall, S.J.

WHERE

In the Education Auditorium (ED 1.100) at the University of Regina, Regina, Saskatchewan.

WHEN

From 1:30 p.m. to 8:30 p.m. on Sunday, December 4th, 1983.

FEES

The registration fee includes 3 panel discussions and coffee breaks.

Registration Fee $10.00
Seniors & Students $ 6.00

PARKING

Participants are permitted to park in any metered area on Sunday at no charge.

FOOD SERVICES

A regular cafeteria style meal may be purchased from 5:15 p.m. - 7:00 p.m. in the College West Cafeteria. Coffee will be provided at the seminar.

For further information contact:
    The Conference Office
    University of Regina
    Room 104, College Building
    Regina, Saskatchewan
    S4S 0A2

(306) 584-4822

THEOLOGY, THIRD WORLD DEVELOPMENT AND ECONOMIC JUSTICE SEMINAR

The Conference Office
University of Regina
Room 104, College Building
Regina, Saskatchewan
S4S 0A2

THEOLOGY, THIRD WORLD DEVELOPMENT AND ECONOMIC JUSTICE
December 4, 1983 — Education Auditorium, University of Regina, Regina, Saskatchewan

☐ I enclose $10.00 registration fee for this one-day seminar. Fee includes 3 panel discussions and coffee break.

☐ I enclose $6.00 registration fee for this seminar. I am a full-time student or a senior citizen.

☐ I would like to make a financial contribution to the University of Regina for the Theology, Third World Development and Economic Justice seminar.

NAME: _____

ORGANIZATION: _____

MAILING ADDRESS: _____

_____ POSTAL CODE _____

TELEPHONE: (BUS) _____ (RES) _____

PLEASE MAKE CHEQUES PAYABLE TO THE UNIVERSITY OF REGINA AND MAIL TO THE CONFERENCE OFFICE,
UNIVERSITY OF REGINA, ROOM 104, COLLEGE BUILDING, REGINA, SASKATCHEWAN S4S 0A2